EDGAR ALLAN POE

EDGAR ALLAN POE

From a copy of the daguerreotype taken about 1849

EDGAR ALLAN POE

A STUDY IN GENIUS

BY

JOSEPH WOOD KRUTCH

NEW YORK

RUSSELL & RUSSELL · INC

1965

To Marcelle

CONTENTS

ILLUSTRATIONS

ILLUSTRATIONS

EDGAR ALLAN POE

I

A GENTLEMAN RATHER THE WORSE FOR WEAR

ON the third of October 1849 a physician of Baltimore, J. E. Snodgrass by name, received from a printer of the same city the following note:

DEAR SIR,

There is a gentleman, rather the worse for wear, at Ryan's 4th ward polls, who goes under the cognomen of Edgar A. Poe, and who appears in great distress, and he says he is acquainted with you, and I assure you he is in need of immediate assistance.

Yours in haste,

JOS. W. WALKER.

As a result of this note the unfortunate man was conveyed to a hospital, given into the care of Dr. J. J. Moran, the resident physician, and suffered to remain there until he died in delirium four days later.

Many years after, both of the physicians concerned joined the eager mob of ladies and gentlemen who, with much internal dissension, were pouring forth their reminiscences of the great and neglected genius whom it had been their privilege to know and who could now bestow upon them both a gleam of reflected glory and the modest remuneration to be received from a newspaper or magazine article. In 1867 Dr. Snodgrass contributed to *Beadle's Monthly The Facts of Poe's Death and Burial*, and in 1885 Dr. Moran produced *A Defense of Edgar*

Allan Poe; Life, Character and Dying Declarations of the Poet in which he described himself as having had the sad privilege of sitting by the poet's deathbed "to administer the cup of consolation; to moisten his parched lip; to wipe the cold death-dew from his brow and to catch the last whispered articulations that fell from the lips of a being, the most remarkable, perhaps, this country has ever known."

The first of these writings has been proved to be entirely untrustworthy and the second, admirably calculated to throw considerable credit upon its author and to embellish the character of the subject, is unfortunately remarkable for two things—first, the unusually clear recollection of events and remarks which one would expect to have been dimmed by the passage of thirty-six years, and, second, the fact that these same minutiae contradict in important particulars what the doctor had said long before he had realized that the man he had attended was to become a hero with a name to defend. In 1885 Dr. Moran remembers, for example, that the poet had "not the slightest odor of liquor upon his breath or person," but in 1849 he had written an account which certainly is at no pains to contradict the obvious implication that his patient was drunk; and there are other similar inconsistencies. From such materials (and they are, unfortunately, as trustworthy as a considerable number of the documents with which the biographer of Poe must concern himself) it is possible to construct a highly romantic legend, but it is not easy to write a sober life.

Fortunately, however, we do possess a letter written by this same doctor to the poet's mother-in-law, Mrs. Clemm, shortly after the events to which it relates took

4

place, and from it we can learn all that we shall ever know concerning this tragic death. It tells us, that is to say, everything of significance concerning the death itself and absolutely nothing of the events which led up to it. From other sources we know that Poe had left Richmond (where he had recently taken a public pledge of temperance) in high spirits a few days previously, and the letter itself informs us that when he was conveyed to the hospital he was unaware of his condition and unable to say who had brought him or with whom he had been associating.

"He remained in this condition from five o'clock in the afternoon—the hour of his admission—until three next morning. . . . To this state succeeded tremor of the limbs, and at first a busy but not violent or active delirium —constant talking—and vacant converse with spectral and imaginary objects on the walls. His face was pale and his whole person drenched in perspiration. We were unable to induce tranquillity before the second day after his admission. . . . I was summoned to his bedside so soon as consciousness supervened, and questioned him in reference to his family, place of residence, relatives etc. But his answers were incoherent and unsatisfactory. He told me, however, he had a wife in Richmond (which I have since learned was not the fact), that he did not know when he had left that city, or what had become of his trunk of clothing. Wishing to rally and sustain his now fast sinking hopes, I told him I hoped that in a few days he would be able to enjoy the society of his friends here, and I would be most happy to contribute in every possible way to his ease and comfort. At this he broke out with much energy, and said the best thing his best friend could do would be to blow out his brains with a pistol—that when he beheld his degradation, he was ready to sink into the earth, etc. Shortly after giving expression to these words, Mr. Poe seemed to doze, and I left him for a short time. When I returned I found him in a violent delirium, resisting the efforts of two nurses to keep him in bed. This state continued until Saturday evening (he was admitted on Wednesday), when he commenced calling for one 'Reynolds,' which he did through the night until *three* on Sunday morning. At this time a very decided change began to affect him. Having become enfeebled from exertion, he became quiet, and seemed to rest for a short time; then gently moving his head, he said, *'Lord help my poor soul!'* and expired. . . . His remains were visited by some of the first individuals of the city, many of them anxious to have a lock of his hair."

Surely this end, as wretched as any in all the annals of literary misery, needs no embellishment, nor is it necessary to call upon the legend which has grown up to explain it. Since Poe was found in a polling place on election day it has been suggested that he was the victim of a gang accustomed to corral strangers and, after intoxicating or drugging them, to use them as voters—a practice quite easy in the absence of any registration system. Poe, so the theory goes, was captured by such a gang and then abandoned upon the streets when the perpetrators of the outrage discovered the violent effect which drink had upon him; but though it is quite possible that something of the sort may have occurred, there is no good reason to believe it beyond a desire to save Poe the disgrace attached to his end, and the events explain themselves without recourse to the legend. During several years immediately preceding his death, the poet's neurotic instability had increased; his actions towards the two women who were engaged to marry him were the actions of a man near madness and his wild utterances concerning the superhuman importance of *Eureka* were the utterances of a man whose egotism had reached the stage of positive delusion. Under the circumstances it is not necessary to call upon any outside agencies to explain his ultimate end, for upon many previous occasions drink had precipitated insanity.

The testimony, it is true, seems to indicate that for some time before leaving Richmond Poe had been sober and had impressed the people with whom he came in contact by his refinement and gentility, but there is in this fact nothing, in the light of his previous life, to cause surprise. A true dypsomaniac in the medical sense, insobriety was with him purely spasmodic, and between the periods when this species of insanity seized him he not only refused alcoholic drink of all kinds but genuinely believed, with the pathetic earnestness of those so affected, that he would never again touch it. Suddenly, however, the fit, the result of some obscure psychic cause, would seize him, he would take one glass, and his balance, perpetually unstable, was hopelessly lost. "During these fits of absolute unconsciousness," he said, "I drank—God only knows how often or how much."

Acquaintances who had seen him only in his normal mind and were, perhaps, on the point of ripening into friends would be amazed by the savage misanthropist into which he was transformed, and when, at last, he came again to himself he would find the position which he had been gradually building for himself in the world completely destroyed. His friends alienated and his job lost, he would be once more an outsider without means for the humblest sustenance, and though he would gradually evolve again some *modus vivendi* it was never for long. Soon he would again fall victim to the strange demon which pursued him.

In all probability, the final catastrophe was begun before he started upon his journey north. On the evening of his departure from Richmond he spent some time in the office of his friend Dr. John Carter and late in the evening he stepped out, taking the doctor's cane, for the avowed purpose of getting his supper at Saddler's, a fashionable restaurant of the time. At Saddler's he met some friends and acquaintances, and according to their testimony he left them sober and cheerful; but Dr. Carter's cane was not returned. Moreover the trunk, the mysterious disappearance of which he could not account for, was left behind at the Swan Tavern in Richmond where he had been staying, and it is hence pretty nearly certain that he left the city in a state of complete irresponsibility. He was provided with a sum of money (estimates vary greatly as to the amount) which he had received as the proceeds of a lecture, and with it he managed to arrive, no one knows just how or when, in Baltimore. There something, probably drink, precipitated a crisis of the chronic inflammation of the meninges from which it is probable he suffered, and he died of it, locking up in himself his secret but ending much as one might have expected him to end and making ridiculous any attempt to consider him as other than a psychopathic case.

Three quarters of a century have passed and the

bibliography of writings about Poe is longer, perhaps, than that devoted to any other American writer except Whitman, and yet from this mountain of matter has emerged no solution of his mystery and no generally accepted estimate of either his work or his character. It is hardly an exaggeration to say that responsible critics have described his writings as little better than trash while others have attempted to raise his name to a position on a level with that of any writer who ever lived. It is equally true that he has, as a man, been represented on the one hand as a fiend and on the other as a gentleman so scrupulous and so respectable as to appear to robust observers an intolerable prig. Making all due allowance for the fact that his actions were so self-contradictory as to make it possible for different observers, seeing him at different times, to form quite different opinions, there remains the inescapable fact that even those who have based their judgment upon the same published works and the same easily available evidence have arrived at the most startlingly divergent opinions. Much of the abysmal sentimentality which he has called forth is no doubt easily explainable, but even discounting all that can be explained there remains the fact that, both as a man and as an artist, Poe was one of those who touch deeply hidden chords and awaken enthusiasms or antipathies which those who feel them cannot logically account for. Baudelaire prayed to him, quite seriously, as a saint, while his most sober biographer could hardly hide, under an effort at scrupulous impartiality, his distaste and confessed to a friend that upon finishing his work he was compelled to pay a visit to Italy to get the taste of Poe out of his mouth.

Though it may not be strange that Professor Wood-berry and Baudelaire should have different tastes, the same differences are observable in the reactions of persons less obviously unlike. In pretty nearly everything written about Poe the *parti pris* is evident. The writer is moved, and he cannot hide the fact that he is appearing somehow for the prosecution or the defense, that he is apologizing for a man who has touched him obscurely to admiration or is justifying a disgust which is not entirely rational. In himself Poe was strange enough but few have been able to describe him without further distortion.

Whatever the nature of this strange trait of his genius, the effect of it upon the formation of his legend began to be evident as soon as his death was known. On October the ninth there appeared in the New York *Tribune* the now famous article which began as surely no death notice ever began before: "Edgar Allan Poe is dead. He died in Baltimore the day before yesterday. This announcement will startle many, but few will be grieved by it. The poet was well known, personally or by reputation, in all this country; he had readers in England, and in several of the states of Continental Europe, but he had no friends."

The author of the article was the Reverend Rufus Griswold, a compiler not without talent whom Poe evidently regarded as a friend and into whose hands he had confided his posthumous fame—at least to the extent of appointing him his editor. After a brief sketch of the poet's life, the errors of which are in part due to the subject's persistent misrepresentation of the facts of his career, the article proceeds to the following passage of extraordinary rhetoric, which, however fanciful it may be, probably represented the impression which Poe had made upon the terrified imagination of the conventional and plodding Griswold.

"His conversation was at times almost super-mortal in its eloquence. His voice was modulated with astounding skill, and his large variably expressive eyes looked repose or shot fiery tumult into theirs who listened, while his own face glowed or was changeless in pallor, as his imagination quickened his blood, or drew it back frozen to his heart. His imagery was from the worlds which no mortal can see but with a vision of genius. . . .

"He was at times a dreamer—dwelling in ideal realms —in heaven or hell, peopled with creations and the accidents of his brain. He walked the streets, in madness or melancholy, with lips moving in indistinct curses or with eyes upturned in passionate prayers, (never for himself, for he felt, or pretended to feel, that he was already damned,) but for their happiness who at that moment were objects of his idolatry; or with his glance introverted to a heart gnawed with anguish, and with a face shrouded in gloom, he would brave the wildest storms; and all night, with drenched garments and arms wildly beating the wind and rain, he would speak as if to spirits that at such times only could be evoked by him from that Aidenn close by whose portals his disturbed soul sought to forget the ills to which his constitution subjected him—close by that Aidenn where were those he loved—the Aidenn which he might never see but in fitful glimpses, as its gates opened to receive the less fiery and more happy natures whose listing to sin did not involve the doom of death. He seemed, except when some

11

fitful pursuit subjected his will and engrossed his faculties, always to bear the memory of some controlling sorrow. The remarkable poem of *The Raven* was probably much more nearly than has been supposed, even by those who were very intimate with him, a reflection and an echo of his own history. He was the bird's

> unhappy master,
> Whom unmerciful disaster
> Followed fast and followed faster
> Till his song the burden bore—
> Melancholy burden bore
> Of 'Nevermore,' of 'Nevermore.'

"Every genuine author in a greater or less degree leaves in his works, whatever their design, traces of his personal character; elements of his immortal being, in which the individual survives the person. . . . But we see here only the better phases of his nature, only the symbols of his juster action, for his harsh experience had deprived him of all faith in man or woman.

"He had made up his mind upon the numberless complexities of the social world, and the whole system was with him an imposture. This conviction gave a direction to his shrewd and naturally unamiable character. Still, though he regarded society as composed of villains, the sharpness of his intellect was not of that kind which enabled him to cope with villainy, while it continually caused him overshots, to fail of the success of honesty. He was in many respects like Francis Vivian in Bulwer's novel of the 'Caxtons.' Passion, in him, comprehended many of the worst emotions which militate against human happiness. You could not contradict him, but you raised quick choler; you could not speak of wealth but

his cheek paled with gnawing envy. The astonishing
natural advantage of this poor boy—his beauty, his readi-
ness, the daring spirit that breathed around him like
a fiery atmosphere—had raised his constitutional self-
confidence into an arrogance that turned his very claims
to admiration into prejudice against him. Irascible, en-
vious—bad enough, but not the worst, for these salient
angles were all varnished over with a cold repellent
cynicism while his passions vented themselves in sneers.
There seemed to him no moral susceptibility; and what
was more remarkable in a proud nature, little or nothing
of the true point of honor. He had, to a morbid excess,
that desire to rise which is vulgarly called ambition, but
no wish for the esteem or love of his species; only the
hard wish to succeed—not shine, not serve,—succeed,
that he might have the right to despise the world which
galled his self-conceit."

In the hands of Poe's admirers Griswold has become,
thanks to this article, a symbol of infamy—the malicious
slanderer of the dead and the dastardly betrayer of one
who had reposed confidence in him—and it is true that
he did in the course of the article repeat some doubtful
stories which, judging Poe as he did, he was too ready
to believe, but in the passage just quoted terror is more
evident than cool or deliberate malice. He had, it is
true, no reason to feel particularly amiable toward his
subject. Poe had quarreled with him as he quarreled
with nearly every man with whom he came in contact;
he had reviled him as sooner or later he reviled nearly
every literary man with whom he had personal relations;
and he was reported to have acted toward Griswold in
a dishonorable manner which, it is pretty clear, did not

seem to his own twisted spirit in any way dishonorable. But Griswold was moved by something more than pure pique. Poe was a figure too strange for his rather limited imagination to grasp or to fit into any human category and he sought refuge from the terror of the inexplicable by transforming Poe into a demon, a creature beyond human explanations.

If Griswold's view were, in essentials, the only prevailing one it would be relatively easy to discount the rhetoric and to form a picture of the man; but as the reader of any of the more idealistic critics of Poe knows, it is quite possible, by the careful selection of facts, to paint a very different picture and to set him forth under a guise almost equally interesting but singularly spotless and pathetic. Griswold was very nearly right in saying that Poe had no friends, if by that we mean men who had known him intimately and long and who could say that their relations with him had been consistently amiable; but there were not lacking those who would resent bitterly the picture which had been drawn. N. P. Willis, who had obtained for Poe one of the many positions which he held for only a brief period, and G. R. Graham, who had also employed him for a time in an editorial capacity, rushed to his defense. Griswold's demon was described as "a quiet, patient, industrious, and most gentlemanly person, commanding the utmost respect and good feeling by his unvarying deportment and ability"; the mad egotist without a spark of honor who hated mankind and had no friends was characterized chiefly by "humility, willingness to persevere, belief in another's kindness, and a capacity for cordial and grateful friendship." "No

RUFUS GRISWOLD

From an engraving

man was more quickly touched by kindness," and he who had been described as believing himself above the duty of fair dealing was "the soul of honor."

Neither the one view nor the other can be discarded as wholly false. In the pages of the present study Poe's heroism will be abundantly clear, and the testimony of those of his immediate family will prove beyond a shadow of a doubt the loving fidelity of which, through indescribable hardships, he was unfailingly capable; but the evidence from which the darker picture draws its colors will be seen to be no less unshakable. Venomous pride, envy, and malice led him to dishonorable acts which no palliation can do more than excuse and we are faced by a man inexplicable by the laws of normal psychology and impossible to defend merely by reference to the difficulties of his career. Since it is impossible to imagine that disease, physical or mental, could account for the presence of goodness in a character essentially evil, we are bound to suppose that a personality so self-contradictory was essentially good; but the presence of a disease which transformed the man cannot be denied, as no ordinary human inconsistency and no ordinary misfortune can account for it. Self-justification is evident in every one of the poet's acts, and he lived in an unreal world which his mind created. To understand that world would be to find the key to his life and to his personality, but without such an understanding nothing can serve to unite the scattered bits into any comprehensible whole. He follows somehow a pattern yet that pattern follows laws which are not the laws of ordinary human character but rather those of some

15

fantastic world as strange yet as self-consistent as the
world in which the creatures of his imagination lead
their nightmare lives.

"Poe," remarked President Hadley of Yale in an attempt to explain the persistent refusal of the committee
to place the poet in the Hall of Fame, "wrote like a
drunkard and a man who is not accustomed to pay his
debts"; and though it is a little difficult to imagine just
what traits of a writer's style can reveal the fact that
his indebtednesses are not promptly liquidated, the silliness of this saying falls short of the silliness of those
who would detach Poe, of all authors, from his work.
It is just the persistent attempt to separate these two
inseparable things which has stood more than anything
else in the way of the complete understanding of either.
Thanks to the fact that the sexual element in his writings is always veiled and was, perhaps, veiled even from
himself, it has been possible for those writings to be
accepted by people who have never understood either the
nature or the origin of the fascination which they exercise
for the simple reason that they have been afraid to do
so. At every step in the investigation of either the
biography or the works, warnings to the timid present
themselves and those bent upon the justification of Poe
have cautiously turned aside from every path that
promised to lead to any fruitful discoveries. The usual
process has been first to whitewash the man as completely
as possible and then, when the impossibility of performing that task in any very satisfactory manner has become evident, to regard the puzzle of his character as
essentially irrelevant, to picture him as a great man unfortunately stained by incidental vices and to imply that

had he possessed a normal nature his work would have been if anything more admirable and more glorious. The result has been to confer upon him finally the reward of a bust in the Hall of Fame and an ode by Mr. Edwin Markham, but the result has also been the continuation of a silly farce in which the most fantastic and abnormal writings in all literature are assumed to be ingenious toys without meaning, and in which the whole process which created them is dismissed as irrelevant.

The most casual consideration is enough to make clear the fact that no more completely personal writer than Poe ever existed. Once when he was employed on a magazine which had decided to change its policy upon the subject of slavery he wrote an article in defense of that institution; once when he was hard pressed for money he wrote a childish article upon a theological question for a religious publication; but aside from these two worthless pieces there are few examples in the whole range of his writings of a single normal interest in the world in which he lived. His one effort to create realistic character (in *The Gold Bug*) was an abysmal failure, and never once did he succeed in describing anything remotely connected with the life about him. There is not, in the ordinary sense, one iota of observation or touch of reality in any story or poem which he produced. No native characters, no observed incidents, no contemporary problems appear; into himself he drew nothing, but he poured out, on the contrary, scenes, characters, and emotions which had no source but his own imagination, no relation to any except the visionary world of which he was the only inhabitant. Yet some of those who profess to admire his work lament his maladjustment to society and speak as though a normal man might by mere exercise of talent have created this complete and terrifying world of fancy in which, as a matter of fact, no man would of his own will choose to live.

Professor Charles W. Kent, a writer typical of those who wish to see in Poe merely an object of pride for all patriotic Americans and, especially, another star in the crown of Old Virginia, remarks of him: "This romantic boy needed most of all the commonplace training of the average boy to save him from the vagaries and eccentricities into which he was falling. It would have been well for him if he could have acquired the steadiness and self-control which he had not inherited. . . . He 'trusted to the fire within' and missed the clear and steady light of the world's best experience." In this connection the obvious comments would seem to be that "the world's best experience" has shown nothing more clearly than the inadvisability of being a poet under any circumstances and that the remark is not particularly applicable to the case of Poe. So nearly identical are the man and his writings that to wish any difference in either the character or experiences of the first is to wish that the other had been different too; and since there is no reason to suppose that Poe would have written at all except as the result of a complete maladjustment to life, that would be also to wish that he had not, as a writer, existed at all. To understand him or his works is, inevitably, to understand them together, and similarly, to accept one is to accept the other. When it was objected to some of his early stories that they were based too much upon morbid German Romanticism Poe replied, the terror which I write "is not of Germany but of the soul"; and that is merely the simple and unescapable truth. Throughout the ensuing study we shall be compelled to assume that the forces which wrecked his life were those which wrote his works.

II

"I AM A VIRGINIAN"

Two conflicting streams of heredity, paralleled by strangely similar streams of experience, met to form the maelstrom which was the personality and career of Poe. Sturdy Irish blood crossed itself with the blood of the strolling player to form the man, and the education of a Virginia gentleman led the way to the career of the shabby outcast. Two inherited bloods and two sets of acquired ideas warred within him, and it is no wonder if the result was chaos.

His grandfather, David Poe, was sometimes referred to as "General Poe of Revolutionary fame," but he had only a slender claim to this distinction. The General's father was an immigrant laborer; he himself had risen from wheelwright to drygoods merchant in the city of Baltimore, and in this capacity he was enabled to supply the Revolutionary Army with clothing; for which service, though he never held any office in the Revolutionary forces, he was known as "Assistant 'Deputy Quartermaster" for his native city and allowed to assume the courtesy title of General. The "General" was a man of that hard and dangerous sort of virtue sometimes called "sturdy," and he was not one to let unworthy tenderness interfere with his principles. Accordingly when a son, also David by name, took it into his head to join a traveling company of players and later to marry an English woman, widow of another member of the troupe, he bothered his head no more about the matter, leaving his degenerate son to shift for himself. When two children had been born of this union and a third was on the way the young man disappeared, either dying at some unknown date, or, as there is some reason for suspecting, deserting his wife; but the General, it would appear, considered both the parents and the children "none of his," for he allowed the infants to be dragged from city to city where the inhabitants had sufficiently forgotten their Puritan prejudices against the stage to applaud a pretty actress but retained sufficient sense of what was due respectability not to concern themselves with the fact that she was dying of hardship and poverty. When finally in Richmond, Virginia, she succumbed to lingering disease some time after the birth of her third child, the General consented to receive the oldest son, William Henry, but allowed the other two children to pass into the hands of charitable strangers.[1] From his father's side Edgar, who had been born in Boston on January 19, 1809, received an inclination towards alcohol afterwards referred to in a letter from a cousin as "the great foe to our family," and from someone, perhaps from his mother, a touch of some darker taint which made his younger sister, Rosalie, a harmless imbecile who was to die many years later in a charitable home; but he got from his family nothing else definable.

Now, chance directed that he should be thrown into a world which neither of his parents and none of his grandparents would have been able to understand.

1 In fairness to General Poe it may be said that Edgar himself afterward stated that his grandfather yielded to the earnest request of the Allans.

To the poor room where his mother had died came
the wife of John Allan, a rising merchant who was
making for himself a place in the hierachy of Southern
society. She decided to take charge of the boy, and
so it was determined that Poe should grow up thinking of himself as a Southern gentleman and yet uneasily
conscious of the fact, often called to his attention,
that he had by birth no right to such a title and that
he held it only by the temporary sufferance of a man
cautious enough to refrain from making any definite
promises or from taking any steps to adopt legally the
youth who was learning the pride of a class in which he
was destined not to remain.

Sentimental biographers have told many doubtful
stories of the foolish indulgences of his foster parents;
they have pictured Poe standing upon a table, wine glass
in hand, pledging the health of admiring guests or
saved from the wholesome discipline of school by the
foolish interference of his protectors; and they have
attempted to explain the vagaries of his career by
making him the conventional spoiled child. But the
true tragedy of his childhood was not so simple; it lay
in the conflict between a pride constantly nourished and
yet continually wounded by a sense that as the son of
an outcast and as a dependent not even sure of his patron
he had no right to it.

The Richmond of the time was, says one of Poe's
schoolfellows, one of the most aristocratic cities on this
side of the Atlantic, and the school to which he was sent
had adopted the prejudices of the community upon which
it drew. The young Poe excelled both in his classes and
in the play field, but it was known to his companions that

his parents had been players and that he was dependent upon the bounty of a stranger. As a result, his fellows refused him the leadership to which his natural capacities entitled him, and his proud nature was wounded continually by slights which were sometimes aggravated by undisguised taunts. At home, too, he found a foster father who was, to say the least, lacking in tact. According to Mrs. Weiss, who drew her information from her mother who had known the family, Mr. Allan had from the first objected to the adoption of Poe because of his actress mother; he was inclined to expect a considerable show of gratitude and he was not above reminding his young ward of his dependence.

The fact that in after years Poe passionately defended the profession of his mother would indicate that he had early learned to hear it spoken of in a slighting manner, and he certainly gave in childhood signs of a temperament which nursed a sense of wrong. All of his schoolfellows who have contributed recollections remark that in spite of his unusual talents he tended to hold himself aloof; one remembers that he was never known to ask a companion to his house, and the reason is not far to seek; Poe was ashamed. Even then he was, in the words of a companion, "self-willed, capricious, inclined to be imperious, and though of generous impulse, not steadily kind or even amiable," exactly as he was in later life. And the reason was, both then and later, that he had all through his life a sense that he was deprived of the preëminence to which his qualities of mind entitled him.

Moreover, the bitterness of this pride was complicated by some other sense of frustration and wrong which sprang from within and which even the most sympathetic of observers could hardly have guessed at the time. Whether the sense of his loneliness drove him back to the memory of the mother whom it was impossible that he should consciously remember or whether some still obscurer cause fixed his imagination upon her, she exercised over his mind a baneful fascination. All his life he carried with him a portrait locket which she had left him; he defended with fierce assertion his pride in her profession; and though there are other reasons why his imagination took a form of horror it is perhaps in some degree because of her that a whole series of his heroines —Ligeia, Berenice, Madeline, and Morella—were wasting away with an inexorable disease. It may have been, also, in part the memory of his mother which made him see in sickness one of the necessary elements of the highest beauty.

It was she too, perhaps, who stood between him and any normal fruition of love. Future events will show how completely absent from his life and his work was anything like normal human passion, and how his inability to feel as other men in this respect increased his sense of frustrated loneliness, but even as a boy this undeveloped conflict helped to set him apart. Once, so the story goes, when the mother of a school acquaintance spoke a kind word to him he fell upon his knees to kiss her hand; and when not long afterwards she died the child, it is said, haunted her grave. Whatever the exact facts upon which this story is based, it was not wholly without foundation, for the memory of Mrs. Stanard, as this lady was called, so haunted his after life that he would tell the story in moments of most intimate confession. Her name, Helen, was to him the magical name,

and when he wished to pay the highest compliment to one
of the living women who for a moment only touched his
imagination, he could think of nothing more fitting to
tell her than that she was mystically destined for him
because her name was the same as that of this shadowy
figure of the past. Thus two dead women ruled his
imagination, and even in boyhood these two women held
him captive. The later events of his life developed to
the full the conflict here begun, but long before he
reached maturity the realization that his desires were
held captive by phantom figures increased both his sense
of isolation and the feeling that he was the victim of
some vague indefinable wrong. "I never knew the time
that Edgar was not in love," said a man who had known
him intimately as a child, and yet there is good reason
to believe that this amorous young man avoided all his
life the sexual connection with any woman.

There is no doubt that Poe was a difficult child, and
the Allan papers, recently investigated for the first time,
make it perfectly clear that the uneasy irritability which
the companions of his later years noted in him and which
they rightly attributed to some inexplicable sense of
wrong had begun to develop very early. The earliest
of the Allan letters refer to the child in terms of pride
and affection, but already in 1824, when Edgar was just
reaching adolescense, his foster father writes a letter full
of disappointment and of a somewhat self-righteous pain
in which he speaks of Edgar's melancholy, of his "moody
and unruly manner toward all the family" for which no
one knows the cause, and of that "complete absence of
any sense of gratitude" of which so many subsequently
complained. Biographers more eager to defend Poe's

character than to understand it have assumed that some fault on the part of Allan must have been wholly responsible for the complete estrangement between him and his foster parent which took place so early in the former's life. But Poe himself was very short tempered, and all that we know of his relationships in later life, all the history of his sudden, violent, and unexpected quarrels with most of the people with whom he came in contact, would lead us to suppose that he was not wholly guiltless. Often in later life he clashed with others because, like most tortured people, he struck out blindly in his pain without stopping to realize that those whom he reviled or wounded were either not responsible for his sufferings or, at least, ignorant of the manner in which they wounded him.

To be sure Allan was not the man (if anyone could have been) to understand the strange creature for whom he had accepted a certain responsibility. He was a hard-headed merchant who was gradually building a fortune for himself in the tobacco business and establishing a place in society which was finally consolidated by an inheritance which made him one of the wealthy men of Virginia. He sent Edgar to school, and he took him on a long business visit to England which extended from 1815 to 1820, but he was not one to sympathize with irrational moods, and probably he did not even realize that his failure legally to adopt the young man to whom he had taught a certain pride was wounding still deeper his self-respect. As the boy grew up moody and sullen, given to quick irrational anger and resentful rather than grateful to the man who was responsible for the anomalous position in which he found himself placed, the latter merely concluded, as there were not wanting others in later life to conclude, that Poe's nature was essentially evil. Yet in 1826, some time after he had moved into a new and imposing home where Poe acquired yet higher ideas of grandeur, Allan was still willing to send the boy for whom he now had no affection to the newly opened University of Virginia and Poe was willing to go. He was old enough to understand clearly by this time his situation as an aristocrat without any assured position, and increasing maturity was making more acute the conflict, which doubtless he did not understand, in his sexual nature; but the University would offer an escape. All the young bloods of Virginia were trooping there, and Jefferson, founder of the University, had carefully omitted any provisions for the discipline of the students in his beloved institution because he believed in the right of the sons of democracy to govern themselves—with the result that the scions of the Virginia aristocracy arrived joyously, and promptly turned the school year into a gentleman's carouse.

The first result of Poe's visit was to stimulate in him more strongly than ever before the haughty and reckless spirit of the old Southern aristocracy. Most of the youths to be found there had been reared in what Philip Alexander Bruce, grave historian of the University and staunch defender of the old order, calls "the open, hearty, and liberal spirit of that life." They had, he says, been riding horses from the time they had sufficient length of leg to bestride one; they had been handling a gun ever since they had had strength to lift stock to shoulder. "From their earliest remembrances, they had seen the full decanter standing on the sideboard ready to give a fillip

27

to the appetite of every male member of the family before dinner was announced or to revive the cheerfulness and renew the vigor of the guest just arrived"; and they had been, moreover, accustomed to other things which Mr. Bruce does not mention—a feudal order of society and a feudal code of conduct. The loyal Southerner, as Professor W. P. Trent has remarked in his biography of William Gilmore Simms, "believed in social distinction and in the respect due to himself by his inferiors. He acknowledged no superiors but as an English gentleman had to defend his honor as zealously as any knight of old." He was, in a word, accustomed to life on the most lavish scale and to the acceptance of privileges without responsibility.

Such an atmosphere was poison to Poe. In it his pride grew apace, in accordance with that regular law which makes those insecure in their position the most punctilious in their insistence upon their privileges and which causes them to be the more intransigent in their demands and more sensitive in their feelings than the proudest of an old aristocracy. Whatever might have been possible for him before, it was now impossible that he should ever reconcile himself to a life of humble labor or fail to feel each slight which he was compelled to bear as an outrage upon one whose right to ease and honor was inherent in his class. If in his future life he was bitter it was as much the aristocrat dispossessed as it was the neglected genius who suffered. "I am a Virginian," he was accustomed to say, and anyone who has ever heard that remark made knows what it means.

Moreover, at the University Poe first learned how reck-

lessness may put pain to temporary flight. The students
at the University had been completely undisciplined;
they gambled, they fought, and they drank; they broke
the windows of the faculty residences, they rang the college bell at outrageous hours, they made their quarters
ring with plantation melodies "not always chaste in dic-
tion or pure in imagery," and they drove blooded horses
tandem through the college grounds. Professors re-
signed, but during the early days the carnival went on.
When doubts assailed Poe as to the permanency of his
position he could stake and lose impressive I. O. U.'s at
cards with a fine recklessness, and when the misery coming from the still deeper source stung him he could, as a
contemporary represents him as doing, drain a glass of
gin at a single gulp—not because he liked the taste but
because he could find in it some forgetfulness. At that
time one glass was all he could take, but it was sufficient,
so this companion informs us, to raise his whole nature
into a state of strong excitement and to produce a torrent
of wild and fantastic talk which held his listeners spell-
bound in amazement. Later Poe learned that though
the desires cannot control the external world they can
build an inward one more real, but in this period he attempted to compensate for his feeling of inferiority by
recklessness and irresponsibility.

These University days were, indeed, the beginning of
the first stage of Poe's lifelong flight from himself. As
a fish, feeling for the first time a hook in his mouth,
rushes wildly away, seeking to convince itself by mad
flight that it is still free until it is brought up with a jerk
at the end of the line, so Poe, by a series of rebellious

29

acts extending over a period of years, sought to deny to himself the fact that circumstances had him in their power and that his line was short.

According to his own statement Poe was allowed to remain at the University only eight months and thus he was soon reminded that he was playing the grand seigneur on sufferance. Mr. Allan plucked him unceremoniously from his aristocratic society and brought him back to Richmond where, tradition has it, he was compelled to undergo the crowning humiliation of humble work in the Allan counting house and where, certainly, his pride must have received some cruel wounds.

The somewhat boyish letters which Poe wrote to his foster father from the University and which sufficiently reveal the tumult of the life there (one of them relates to the expulsion of a fellow-student for severely biting his antagonist in a fight) seem to assume the resumption of a friendly interest on the part of Mr. Allan, but extensive debts were the immediate cause of Poe's downfall. Tradition has it that they were debts of honor in the conventional sense of the phrase, but there were certainly other debts too. Poe confessed to improper conduct and some time later Mr. Allan wrote: "He left me in consequence of some gambling at the University at Charlottesville, because (I presume) I refused to sanction a rule that the shopkeepers and others had adopted there, making Debts of Honor of all indiscretions"; and among the recently published documents mentioned before are several dunning letters, some addressed to Poe and some to Allan personally, requesting payment of various sums. One, since it shows that Edgar had already adopted the somewhat cavalier manner in dealing with money matters which was one of his mature characteristics, is worth quoting.

"When I saw you in Richmond a few days ago," it reads, "I should have mentioned the difference between us if there had not been so many people present. I must, of course, as you did not mention it to me, inquire of you if you ever intend to pay it. If you have not the money write me word that you have not, but do not be perfectly silent. I should be glad if you would write to me even as a friend. There can certainly be no harm in your avowing candidly that you have no money if you have none, but you can say when you can pay me if you can't now. I heard when I was in Richmond that Mr. Allan would discharge all your debts. If it was a gambling debt I should not think much of it. But under the circumstances I think very strangely of it. Write me upon the receipt of this letter and tell me candidly what is the matter." Another from a gentleman in Charlottesville presses a charge of $6.25 for a slave used by Poe and still another from a haberdasher indicates that the Poe who spent most of the rest of his life in shabby black was, in the words of Professor Killis Campbell, at this period "a disciple, in matters of dress, of Bulwer or the younger Disraeli." He was, it is always necessary to bear in mind if one is to understand his complicated bitterness, a Bohemian from necessity and by no means from choice.

To be denied the extravagance with which he was soothing his pride and to be publicly humiliated before the people of Richmond was more than Poe could bear. Suddenly he left the Allan home, after some quarrel the immediate cause of which we do not know, and, doubtless feeling for the moment that to hide his shame would bring him some relief, he enlisted in Boston on May 26, 1827 in the United States Army, thus performing an act so utterly mad as to prove beyond any possible doubt that suffering had banished judgment. Professor Harrison, anxious as always to account for Poe's qualities by the external circumstances of his life, offers the remarkable suggestion that ".the precision of the army routine had something to do with the growing precision of Poe's style," and that "his intense feeling for rhythm may have been encouraged by the measured tread of the soldiers' feet"; but it is difficult for those gifted with a less romantic imagination to believe that he found in the barracks anything but a deeper humiliation, and certainly he himself seems rapidly to have concluded that even Allan's niggardly patronage was better than no patronage at all. To Allan he wrote humble letters begging passionately for a reconciliation and, after much delay, secured through his foster father a transfer to West Point where, on July 1, 1830 he was matriculated as a cadet.

In later life Poe learned to live in an imaginary world, to deny the actual facts which disturbed him and to accept the picture of himself which his desire created as the real one, failing of some sort of an adjustment to life only when the action of some other person violated the tradition of his dream world. But, as has already been indicated, he had not at this early period learned wholly to deny facts, and he was constantly searching for some manner of life which would enable him to maintain himself in a position which satisfied in its outward circumstances his pride. West Point was doubly a forlorn hope, and Poe, who had already definitely revealed his literary ambition, doubtless had little temperamental inclination toward the army; but the career of an officer was still, according to the Virginia tradition, the career of a gentleman, and all his life long Poe wanted to be some kind of a gentleman quite as much as he wanted to be a genius—indeed, as will be made evident, he valued literary achievement chiefly as a means of giving to himself the right to scornful pride which birth and social position had failed to give him.

It is possible that he hoped, too, that at the military academy he might reëstablish himself in Mr. Allan's favor and finally succeed to his place and fortune, but it was a desperate hope because the letter which Mr. Allan wrote to secure the appointment was singularly cold; one phrase which it contained would certainly seem to indicate that he had definitely abandoned any intention he might once have had of making Poe his heir. "Frankly sir," he wrote to the Honorable John H. Eaton, Secretary of War, "do I declare that he is no relation to me whatsoever; that I have many in whom I have taken an active interest to promote theirs, with no other feeling than that, every man is my care, if he be in distress." From this it is evident that Allan wished as far as possible to forget that none of those of whom he spoke in these cold lines had been received by him in his house as a son. There is, of course, no reason to suppose that Poe ever saw this letter, and since another letter from one of his old Army officers speaks of "an entire reconciliation on the part of Mr. Allan, who receives him into his family and favor," it is quite possible that Poe was ignorant of the exact nature of his foster father's feeling; though he was soon to realize that the hopes which he was again building of a secure place in society were without foundation.

Mrs. Allan, who was responsible for Poe's reception into the Allan household and who had probably been all along his chief protector, had died on February 28, 1829, and on October 5, 1830 her husband married again. Doubtless Poe realized that this second marriage, with its promise (soon fulfilled) of a natural heir to the Allan fortune, was the death of all his hopes; and he set out to extricate himself from the position in which he had placed himself and from which he could now gain nothing, since he had no desire for the life of an army officer without private fortune and without influence.

There is no doubt that his expulsion from West Point on March 6, 1831 was the result of a definite plan. That he was not incapable of discipline is proved both by the good record which he made as a common soldier and by the fact that he had got himself into no previous difficulties at the Academy. On January 5, 1831 a Court Martial had been convened to try cadet offenders, and after a single setting adjourned until January 28. For two weeks preceding this second sitting Poe neglected practically all his duties as a cadet and was summoned, as a matter of course, to answer a number of charges. He had previously written Mr. Allan begging the necessary permission to resign and the fact that he pleaded guilty to all the specifications except the one—absence from parade, roll call, and guard duty—which could not be successfully denied, proves that he deliberately sought his dismissal and that his expulsion was, so far as he was concerned, merely a resignation.

Shortly afterwards Poe went to Baltimore and commenced the second period of his life, the period in which he began to build up the legend of himself and attempted

to make some adjustment between the demands of his ego
and a worldly situation which in no wise satisfied him;
but his life touched the Allans again, and since that contact really belongs to the first period, it should be included here as the end of the first chapter of his life.
Shortly before Allan's death on March 27, 1834 Poe,
who had, it seems, been in the house but once before since
he entered West Point, called upon him and according
to one account forced his way into his foster father's
bedroom. It is barely possible that even at this late date,
and in spite of the fact that children had come to absorb
Mr. Allan's affection, Poe still had some faint hope of
receiving further help from him; but it is much more
likely that, realizing that he had nothing more to gain,
Poe wished merely to enjoy the emotional luxury of a
quarrel in which he could give free and refreshing vent
to feelings which he had previously been compelled more
or less to repress.

Concerning the circumstances of this last home-coming,
as concerning the circumstances of so many other events
in Poe's life, we are compelled to say that there remains
considerable doubt. The niece of the second Mrs. Allan
writes as follows: "She [Mrs. Allan] told me that Poe
had never been to their home but twice and she only saw
him once. It was when her eldest son was three weeks
old. He came upstairs to her bedroom, and began in an
abusive manner to rail at herself and baby. She asked
her nurse to ring the bell. It was answered by the butler,
and she said: 'James, put this drunken man out of the
house,' which he did. The next time he visited the house
must have been about four years afterwards, for it was
during the last illness of Mr. Allan. He was sitting in

a large chair trying to read a newspaper when the door opened, and Poe came in. Mr. Allan became very much excited, shook his cane at him, and ordered him out of the house, using very strong language, for he had never forgiven him, and whether he came to plead forgiveness, or to upbraid, no one knew, since the old gentleman did not give him a chance to say a word."

If we add to this story another, well vouched for, which tells how Poe on a visit to the Allans quarreled with the second Mrs. Allan, a lady of great social ambitions who wished to slight him and indicated her attitude by putting him to sleep in a servant's room, and if we add also Poe's own statement: "I gave up the prospect of a large fortune rather than bear a trivial wrong," we shall not, it is true, have any very clear idea exactly what happened; but we shall perceive the essential fact, which is that the last hope of real friendship between him and Mr. Allan was killed when he left West Point and that these later visits have nothing more than an emotional significance. Poe's knowledge of an Allan secret made any reconciliation impossible and by the time Poe was twenty-five years old he had succeeded in completely destroying all the prospects which he had had as a child. He was occupying a very humble position in the city where he had promised to become one of the leaders of a proud society, and far from shining he was not only penurious but in some measure disgraced. The real world would have none of him, and his own flight was into the world where dreams count as facts and where, also, alas, shadowy horrors become no less real than shadowy triumphs.

Doubtless Mr. Allan must bear his share in the blame for the wreck which even at this early period had been

JOHN ALLAN

From a portrait in the Allan House, Richmond, Va.

made of Poe's career as a man as distinguished from his career as an artist. Allan seems, indeed, to have grown coarser with the years and there was a scandal in his life which the owners of his papers still refuse to allow to be made public; but the burden cannot be wholly shifted to him. The highly important documents just issued under the title of *Edgar Allan Poe Letters Till Now Unpublished in the Valentine Museum, Richmond Virginia* make clear many things concerning these early years but they make nothing more clear than the extraordinary instability of Poe's character. His denunciations of Allan alternate during a period of years with attempts at reconciliation and he shows himself already a man with whom it was almost impossible to deal. When he left Richmond to join the army he declared himself forever free from Allan and in the same letter requested money; when he was asking aid in getting himself transferred to West Point he declared that he "never meant to offer a shadow of excuse for the infamous conduct of myself and others" at the University and yet sometime later he attempts to disclaim all responsibility with the words: "I will boldly say that it was wholly and entirely your own mistaken parsimony that caused all the difficulties in which I was involved at Charlottesville."

It is impossible not to conclude from the evidence of these letters that Poe was one of that class of persons so immersed in their own misery as to be absolutely incapable of understanding the psychology of those upon whom they are dependent and who, in consequence, expect a sudden submission to wipe out all memory not only of past transgression but of the fact that similar submissions and similar promises have often enough before come to nothing. Even as late as 1833 Poe was still appealing for money and he had certainly received money long after Allan had ceased to have any hopes whatever for him. At the same time that the last appeal was received Poe's foster father indorsed a previously received letter with the following words and he may well have believed them justified. "It is now upwards of 2 years since I received the above precious relict of the Blackest Heart and deepest ingratitude alike destitute of honor and principle every day of his life has only served to confirm his debased nature— Suffice it to say my only regret is in Pity for his failings—his Talents are of an order that can never prove a comfort to their possessor." Poe, it must be remembered, had not at this time given any evidence of genius and he had given ample evidence of ungovernable passions. If, as I assume to be the case, Allan had contributed to the ruin of Poe's character by first consciously and then unconsciously torturing his pride with allusions to his origin and his dependent state, at least that ruin was complete long before Allan utterly cast him off.

If in this very brief sketch of Poe's earliest years I do not seem to have availed myself even to a legitimate extent of the biographer's privilege by virtue of which he may defend his hero and palliate the less admirable aspects of his career and character, it is not because I have wished to wrong the man whom life wronged enough, and who certainly suffered more than any man deserves to suffer, but because I would rather see him as a consistent whole than take advantage of the obscurity of his earlier years to lay all the blame upon others—only to be compelled in the discussion of subsequent events to admit that the cause of Poe's defects lay not more in others than in himself. If the child was father to the man then the child was, as those who knew him have represented, moody, melancholy, and not seldom unreasonable to the last degree.

Moreover, to regard the young Poe as merely the victim of an unjust man is to deprive ourselves of any power of understanding the background of ideas which can alone make clear the logic of his actions or explain the origin of the nameless horror that haunted him or the insane thirst for renown which made him say: "I love fame. I dote upon it. I idolize it. I would drink to the dregs the glorious intoxication; I would have incense arise in my honor from every hamlet."

"MY PASSIONS WERE ALWAYS OF THE HEAD"

THE months which lie between March 1831, when Poe was expelled from West Point, and the summer of 1833, when his prize-winning story gave him his first touch of literary fame, are months of obscurity. During at least a part of the period he lived, as we now know, with his aunt Mrs. Clemm, a seamstress of Baltimore, and we do not know whether or not he was wholly dependent upon her bounty. Stories, based apparently upon fact, have come to us of two flirtations, one with a cousin and another with a neighbor who is the Mary of some of his verses, but the mental processes of the period, evidently of great importance, are unknown. His pride must have had, during this time, little enough on which to feed itself, for his dream of gentlemanly self-sufficiency was gone and he had not yet begun to establish the legend which sustained him. In 1831 he wrote a letter, humbler than any which he ever brought himself to write afterward, to an acquaintance of Baltimore begging for some employment "in which salary would not be the first consideration," but even were it not for this letter there is another fact which testifies more eloquently than spoken words to the humiliation of this period. Never in all his life did Poe admit that the obscure hiatus had existed.

When his fame had reached a point where biographical details were called for he invented a story of a romantic expedition to Europe in the interests of Greek freedom, and told in all seriousness of some difficulties in Russia which put an end to his heroic experience and necessitated his return to America in time to receive his first modest triumph. In all the early accounts of his life this silly story is repeated, and even upon what he believed his deathbed he is said to have reiterated it. Hardship and romantic wrong were a part of the necessary color of his legend, but he could never bring himself to admit that for more than two years he had been not a distinguished man hated and persecuted by his fellows but merely the obscure recipient of humble charity. To no one did he ever confess the truth, and so well did he keep it hid that even as late as 1880 the first important biography of him repeats this story and its author speculates, after the manner of biographers, upon the probable effect of the European scene upon his imagination. When his legend was in question Poe had no scruples concerning the truth, and he even invented the story of a novel which was written during this period, printed in France, and attributed to Eugene Sue!

In the summer of 1833 a publication of Baltimore called *The Saturday Visiter* announced a literary contest planned upon a scale not particularly munificent. For the best short story it offered fifty dollars, for the best poem twenty-five, and it specified, in addition, that all manuscripts submitted should become the property of the magazine, thus providing itself with a considerable quantity of literary material in return for the two modest prizes. The jury consisted of John P. Kennedy, the novelist, James H. Miller, and J. H. B. Latrobe, editor of the paper. To them Poe submitted a group of stories called *Tales of the Folio Club* and a poem, *The Coliseum.* Though he was unknown to the judges they awarded him without discussion the short story prize and would have given him the other also had it not been for a natural reluctance to give both to the same person. *The Coliseum* was published some time later, and for it, presumably, Poe received no material payment.

Recent investigation has dulled a little the drama of Poe's sudden triumph by revealing the fact that previous to this he had published anonymously several stories in newspapers; but this was nevertheless his first taste of the sweets of renown. Already the dream of compensating for his wounded pride by achieving literary fame had occurred to him, and he was not slow to seize the opportunity now offered him to form literary acquaintances. Immediately after the publication of his prize-winning tale, *MS. Found in a Bottle,* Poe appeared in the office of the editor, and the recollection of the latter gives us our first sight of his mature appearance.

"He was, if anything, below the middle size, and yet could not be described as a small man. His figure was remarkably good, and he carried himself erect and well, as one who had been trained to it. He was dressed in black, and his frock coat was buttoned to the throat, where it met the black stock, then almost universally worn. Not a particle of white was visible. Coat, hat, boots, and gloves had very evidently seen their best days, but so far as mending and brushing would go everything had been done, apparently, to make them presentable. On most men his clothes would have looked shabby and seedy, but there was something about this man that pre-

vented one from criticizing his garments, and the details
I have mentioned were only recalled afterwards. The
impression made, however, was that the award in Mr.
Poe's favor was not inopportune. *Gentleman* was written all over him. His manner was easy and quiet, and
although he came to return thanks for what he regarded
as deserving them, there was nothing obsequious in anything he said or did. His features I am unable to describe in detail. His forehead was high, and remarkable
for the great development at the temple. This was the
characteristic of his head, which you noticed at once, and
which I have never forgotten. The expression of his
face was grave, almost sad, except when he was engaged
in conversation, when it became animated and changeable. His voice, I remember, was very pleasing in its
tone and well modulated, almost rhythmical, and his
words were well chosen and unhesitating."

It is obvious that even at this time Poe did not forget the dignity which was so important to him, and obvious too that he had already assumed the pose of a man
versed in strange learning, for he spoke of *A Voyage
to the Moon* upon which he was engaged and he went
at once into "a somewhat learned disquisition upon the
laws of gravity, the height of the earth's atmosphere, and
the capacity of balloons, warming in his speech as he proceeded." His poverty Poe hardly wished to hide, for
from these men he expected help, but he wished also to
impress them with two things: first, that he was no mere
needy scribbler but a gentleman as well as a genius, and
second, that behind that impressive forehead which could
not but be noticed was a store of learning (in which he

himself almost believed) which enabled him to penetrate mysteries closed to ordinary mortals. As he talked of esoteric things he became more and more excited. He "spoke so rapidly, gesticulating much, that when the turn up-side-down took place, and he clapped his hands and stamped with his foot by way of emphasis, I was carried along with him, and, for ought to the contrary that I now remember, may have fancied myself the companion of his aërial journey— When he had finished his description he apologized for his excitability, which he laughed at himself." Doubtless Poe himself did not realize for the moment where truth stopped and imagination began. The hidden springs of his imagination were touched and he was borne aloft, far away from the actualities of the moment, in a vision which was at once an escape and a fulfillment. For once the flight was without its penalty. He came safely to earth again without descending, as he almost always did descend, into some region more terrible than the reality from which he was fleeing.

Poe's small success in winning the *Visiter* prize did not bring him the good fortune which he hoped. This journal announced its intention of publishing by subscription the other *Tales of the Folio Club*, but the plan was abandoned at Poe's own request and the stories sent off to a publisher by whom they were, in the end, rejected. Yet the impression which he had made upon the judges was not lost. After a short visit to Richmond, during which the visit to Mr. Allan (previously referred to) took place, he returned to Baltimore and on March 15, 1835 pleaded with Mr. Kennedy, through whom also he had sold at least one story to an annual, for help in obtaining a position as schoolmaster. Kennedy replied with an invitation to dinner and received in return a note which reads:

DEAR SIR:
Your kind invitation to dinner today has wounded me to the quick. I cannot come—and for reasons of the most humiliating nature—my personal appearance. You may conceive my deep mortification in making this disclosure to you—but it was necessary. If you will be my friend so far as to loan me $20, I will call on you tomorrow—otherwise it will be impossible, and I must submit to my fate.
Sincerely,
Yours,
E. A. POE.

As a result of this note, Kennedy says "I gave him clothing, free access to my table, and the use of a horse for exercise when he chose; in fact, brought him up from the verge of despair." Thanks to Kennedy also Poe sold a story to the newly founded *Southern Literary Messenger* of Richmond and presently became editor of that magazine at a salary of $520 a year.

September 1835 found him modestly established in a boarding house in Richmond and thus once more upon the scene of his youthful hopes. He writes exultantly that his friends have received him with open arms but it was nevertheless upon a very different footing that he had come back. Mr. Allan was dead and Poe had not the slightest chance of regaining the position which he had once had. He was now only a humble journalist. According to Mrs. Weiss he was, during this period, disappointed in his hope to take his old place in Richmond society since, because of the scandal connected with him, he was shunned and it was even said that when one of the social leaders, the mother of Mrs. Julia Mayo Cabell, gave an entertainment to which he was invited, two of his former schoolmates refused to attend.

Shortly the *Messenger* was to leap into a considerable fame and the name of Poe was to become known as that of a haughtily severe critic as well as of the author of strange and terrible tales. Later, too, stories of wild intemperance, ungovernable temper, and cynical opinions not fully expressed but smacking of misanthropy and atheism, were to give their subject a lurid fame and to mark him as a man who despised his fellows as much as he surpassed them. He was, indeed, to take in this sinister reputation a certain satisfaction but at the present the young author was only again a victim to the irrational melancholy and the vague fears which pursued him. Others might shudder with the delight of a purely literary horror at the tales which he wrote but he was compelled to suffer the tortures from which they sprang.

On September 11, he wrote to J. P. Kennedy: "The situation is agreeable to me for many reasons—but alas! it appears to me that nothing can now give me pleasure —or the slightest gratification. Excuse me, my Dear Sir, if in this letter you find much incoherency. My feelings at this moment are pitiful indeed. I am suffering under a depression of spirits such as I have never felt before. I have struggled in vain against the influence of this melancholy.—I say you will believe me, and for this simple reason, that a man who is writing for *effect* does not write thus. My heart is open before you—if it be worth reading, read it. I am wretched and know not why. Console me—for you can. But let it be quickly—or it will be too late." Nothing in the letter hints at the cause of this depression, and Poe himself did not know what it was but for the first time we have his own confession—many times later repeated—that he suffered from causes unknown. Spectres haunted him, and he described in morbidly beautiful prose their form and effect but he could neither lay nor understand them.

Scarcely had he settled himself in his new duties when he became the victim of one of the recurrent fits of intemperance which seized him, and he was on the verge of losing permanently his newly found position. "No man," wrote Mr. White, proprietor of the *Messenger*, "who drinks before breakfast is safe," and Poe who had left Richmond when this letter was written wrote a reply but we have only White's response to it from which a paragraph or two will bear quotation.

"Would that it were in my power," writes Mr. White, "to unbosom myself to you, in language such as I could on the present occasion wish myself master of. I cannot do it—and therefore must be content to speak to you in my plain way.

"That you are sincere in all your promises, I firmly believe. But Edgar, when you once again tread these streets, I have my fears that your resolves would fall through—and that you would again sip the juice, even till it stole away your senses. Rely on your own strength, and you are gone! Look to your Maker for help, and you are safe!

"How much I regretted parting with you, is unknown to anyone on earth except myself. I was attached to you—and am still—and willingly would I say return,

47

if I did not dread the hour of separation very shortly again.

"If you could make yourself contented to take up your quarters in my family, or in any other private family where liquor is not used, I should think there were hopes for you.—But if you go to a tavern, or to any other place where it is used at table, you are not safe. I speak from experience.

"You have fine talents, Edgar,—and you ought to have them respected as well as yourself. Learn to respect yourself, and you will very soon find that you are respected. Separate yourself from the bottle, and bottle-companions, forever.

"Tell me if you can and will do so,—and let me hear that it is your fixed purpose never to yield to temptation.

"If you should come to Richmond again, and again should be an assistant in my office, it must be expressly understood by us that all engagements on my part would be dissolved, the moment you get drunk."

Poe's reply is lost, but shortly after that he returned to Richmond in the company of Mrs. Clemm and her young daughter Virginia. When the issue of the *Messenger* for December 1835 appeared it bore the name of Poe as editor and continued to do so until another outbreak of intemperance permanently severed his connection with the magazine.

There has been occasion before this to allude more than once to Poe's tendency toward the occasional immoderate use of alcohol but this letter from Mr. White is the first of a series of similar glimpses which we get of the effect of this weakness upon his career and it is necessary to dispose once and for all of the subject which has been unfortunately made the center of most discussions of Poe. It appears to explain his defects, and it has afforded an admirable talking point to both his defenders and his enemies, constituting either a conclusive damnation of himself and his work or a complete excuse for all his short-comings. This fact is the result, perhaps, of our national tendency to regard alcohol as the ultimate source of all evil but it requires but little investigation of the facts to show that, in itself, Poe's drunkenness explains nothing.

As a boy in Richmond he had been raised in a society of hard drinkers or, as Mr. Bruce more delicately puts it, "there were never kinder and more generous men and women than those composing the refined and cultivated circle in which he had moved in Richmond; there the mint julep and the apple toddy were passed around, not so much for the gratification of an appetite, as for the expression of good will and good fellowship." Thus Poe became early acquainted with the relief which alcohol can bring. But to seek no further for the cause of Poe's drunkenness would be to neglect two important facts, first, that some hundreds of other boys who grew up apparently under the same circumstances led sober lives, and second, that Poe's drinking was distinctly not of the social kind. Unquestionable testimony from many sources proves that there were long periods during which he would touch nothing, and all who knew him during a considerable period of time insist that he was not a steady drinker but that the fit seized him as a sort of madness which transformed his own character and made him almost unrecognizable to his friends. "It has not," he told Mrs. Whitman, "been in pursuit of pleasure that I have periled life and reputation and reason. It has been in the desperate attempt to escape from torturing memories, from a sense of insupportable loneliness, and a dread of some strange impending doom." In his letters he more than once makes a similar statement and there is every reason to believe that it is essentially true. Between these fits which came upon him he could never understand why he had behaved as he had, and repeated over and over again, with the pathetic confidence of the pathological drunkard, that his weakness had been completely conquered and that there was no danger of his ever yielding to it again. Sooner or later, however, the moment would again arrive, the fit would seize him, and his friends, as he once complained, would make the mistake of attributing the insanity to the drink instead of the drink to the insanity.

Dr. John W. Robinson in a book devoted to the study of Poe's intemperance and called *Edgar A. Poe: A Study*, compares all the evidence and proves beyond any question that Poe was a true dypsomaniac, one, that is to say, whose drunkenness, sporadic and apparently inexplicable, is the result of a diseased soul, but he makes no attempt to answer the most interesting and only really significant question: What was the cause of that disease? Drunkards do not laboriously produce strangely beautiful and profoundly morbid literature; but that "dread of some strange impending doom" which Poe speaks of as the cause of his drinking must certainly have played a part in the stories and poems so full of a strange irrational terror. If we could get, not at the facts, but at the *cause* of the intemperance we might at least have some inkling of the secret of his genius.

I have already spoken of the rôle which wounded pride doubtless had in producing his wild career at the University of Virginia, and have spoken also of certain psychic difficulties from which Poe had doubtless already begun to suffer at that period, but there occurred at the stage of his life which we have just been discussing an event which throws a flood of light upon his mental state.

Scarcely was Poe well settled in his new home when he was married to Virginia Clemm, a girl who was not only literally a child in years but was destined to remain all her life a child in mind. She was the daughter of the woman who had sheltered him in Baltimore, he had known her almost since her infancy, and she had acted as a childish confidante during the course of one of the flirtations of his obscure years. Now he married her, and to whatever reasons one may attribute the act they cannot but suggest something abnormal. As early as September 22, 1834 when the child had just completed her twelfth year he had taken out a license to marry her in Baltimore but the strenuous and understandable objections of a distant relative either postponed the wedding or kept it a secret. Mrs. Clemm, however, a simple-minded woman who was devoted with an absolutely unquestioning devotion to Poe, supported him in this as she supported him in everything else that he wished to do and now on May 16, 1836 the pair were publicly and religiously married in Richmond by a Presbyterian minister to whom the bride "seemed very young" in spite of the fact that an acquaintance of Poe's obligingly perjured himself by declaring that Virginia was of the full legal age of twenty-one years.

Poe's love affairs, both before and after this one, were

usually somehow fantastic. Generally they were purely "platonic" like his boyhood worship of Mrs. Stanard, but when they tended to approach the physical they were frenetically violent. In later years, as we shall see, he went completely mad when passion touched him, and once before his marriage he had shown how dangerous love in the ordinary sense was to his mental stability. During the obscure Baltimore period he had begun a flirtation with "Mary" (recently identified as a certain Miss Devereux) and late one evening he suddenly proposed that they be married upon the instant. Startled, she refused, but not long after he appeared at her home intoxicated and behaved in a manner so insanely violent that he was forbidden the house. The incident was prophetic of the character of his conduct during a whole series of brief love affairs late in life, but none of these strange affairs was so strange as his marriage, which was, it appears, no real marriage, with the child Virginia.

The event is indeed one very difficult of explanation for those who are loath to admit that the abnormality of Poe's literary expression had its roots in the very center of his being. Such persons tend to undertake the impossible task of making this marriage romantic. Sentimentalists stress the undoubted fact that Poe was always devoted to his wife in a brotherly fashion, and they have even suggested that this extraordinary union with a child is additional proof of the remarkable purity of his character; but facts cannot be denied. If it was his intention to make her fully his wife his act strongly suggests either abnormality or brutality, and if, as was certainly the case, he intended her as a wife in name

EDGAR ALLAN POE
From a painting by Samuel S. Osgood

only, this deliberate renunciation of a normal life cannot but indicate the existence of some emotional disturbance of profound importance in any understanding of the nature of the strange productions of his imagination. Here is a man who was always, as one who knew him said, in love. His entire life from childhood to death was an almost unbroken series of hectic and abortive flirtations; and yet, at the very beginning of his career, he deliberately tied himself to a child with whom for some time, at least, after the marriage was arranged sexual relations would be impossible.

It so happened that prolonged illness made sexual relations with her impossible even after she reached maturity and it may be suggested that certain of Poe's psychic abnormalities were a result of the unnatural restraint that he was called upon to exercise; but in view of his temperament and his actions such an explanation seems to me to be essentially inaccurate and superficial. Poe, it is true, could not have known that Virginia would become a permanent invalid but he certainly did know when he proposed to marry a girl just over twelve that the marriage must remain for some time at least unconsummated. It must have been the sexlessness of her beauty which appealed to him and thus a temporary continence was not so much thrust upon him as deliberately chosen. Doubtless he was aware in his own mind of nothing except the charm which feminine beauty divorced from any suggestion of conscious sex had for him and he would call his admiration for Virginia a worship of purity: but when we consider the distaste which his writings reveal for the whole idea of sexual passion and the unhappy history of his constantly frustrated flirtations with other women we may guess that this abnormal absorption in purity was but one of the outward signs of a deep-lying inhibition and we may guess also the function which Virginia was to perform in his life, though he himself did not clearly understand the fascination which she had for him. Her youth would serve as an excuse for leaving her untouched and the fact that he was already married would furnish him a plausible reason why all his affairs with other women must remain, if not exactly platonic, at least unconsummated. Events to be discussed later will make it clear that the efforts to escape from a realization of his own condition was part of one of the essential processes of Poe's life, but no act reveals more clearly than this one both his abnormality and the fact that he was desperately determined that it should not be admitted even to himself.

Mrs. Susan Weiss, a member of the large company of female Poe-worshippers, endeavors to explain the whole affair by maintaining that Poe was no more than a passive victim and that the marriage was merely a trick (of which Poe made the sorry best he could) on the part of Mrs. Clemm, who wished above all else a firm hold upon the irresponsible young man to whom she had become so firmly attached. The suggestion is, in the light of Poe's adoring attitude toward his wife, highly fantastic, but it does nevertheless give an obvious suggestion of one side of the truth, which is that he did deliberately marry the mother almost as much as he married the daughter. Though he did not need women in the way that normal men need them, he was extraordinarily dependent upon them for two things—inspiration and care. Virginia, described as "like a Canova" at the time when that was considered a compliment, perfectly met the needs of his morbid imagination because her undeveloped mind and pale unhealthy face, with the high forehead characteristic of the family, satisfied his conception of an unearthly purity. But she had neither the intelligence even to feign a sympathetic interest in his work nor the practical capacity to give him the maternal care which he had to have. Poe did not hesitate in after years to use the women who were fascinated by his personality for his material advantage, and there is no reason to suppose that he failed to see the advantage to himself in drawing yet more close the capable and devoted mother whom he would acquire with his wife. Thus his marriage may, with little exaggeration, be described as a double one. In Mrs. Clemm he both loved and used the mother whose Shadow haunted him; in Virginia he had bodily before his eyes that consumptive angel who figures in all his dreams. They were ghostly shadows whose unreality seemed to make unnecessary the physical union which he could not offer.

The judgments passed upon Virginia's physical appearance vary considerably. Some speak of her as a dream of loveliness, and if one may judge from her picture she must have seemed, as she sat beside her harp in all the unimportant purity of an undeveloped mind, the very ideal of Victorian maidenhood as we see it represented in the sentimental engravings of the period. But those who have left descriptions of her seem to indicate that she was less beautiful than strange. Her dark hair and violet eyes were set off by an expression that was a genuine reflection of her sweet and affectionate disposition, but the height of her forehead spoiled the symmetry of her face and her complexion was so completely pale as to be described by some as "pure white" and by others as merely "bad." None deny, however, that her mind was absolutely undeveloped and that the combination of dark hair, bright eyes, and unearthly whiteness gave her the appearance of something not quite human. As she grew older she became not a little plump, but she grew older only in body, and the lisping speech which issued from her pouting lips expressed the childishness of her mind.

There can be no doubt that she herself was blindly devoted to Poe and that her existence like that of her mother revolved about him. It is said that she idolized him even at the time when they were first thrown together in Baltimore, and she idolized him until her death, but her devotion was, in the words of a woman who knew the Poe ménage, the same which she would have given "to a greyhound or any other handsome pet", and the affection which he returned was of the same slightly unreal sort. We see her fetching from the desk and then unfolding in delight before a visitor one of the long scrolls upon which her husband wrote, but it was to her no more than a toy, and it was with the mother that Poe discussed both his artistic and practical affairs.

Their marriage remained, throughout, singularly incomplete, spiritually as well as physically. Significantly enough the endearing name by which he always referred to her was merely "Sis," and in all of the voluminous correspondence which has been preserved only one of his letters is addressed to her; for when he wished to communicate with her he always addressed her through her mother as he might have addressed a child. Even at the beginning of his married life he was accustomed to go into society without her, and when toward the end he began to appear in literary drawing-rooms it was usually alone. If she came with him it was only to sit in perfect silence, and when he entered upon one of his tragi-comic flirtations toward the end of his life there was from her no sign of jealousy. She was, in all probability, ignorant of what flirtation means.

"I believe," said Mrs. Frances S. Osgood, who knew him well, "that she [Virginia] was the only woman whom he ever loved," and this is substantially true since he was incapable of loving in any complete sense. To a friend he wrote wishing him as great a happiness in marriage as his own had been, and he spoke of Virginia as the sole support of his life; he clung to her desperately, and after she had died his life went into complete collapse; but it was not because he loved her with the love of a husband for his wife. She was the means by which he sublimated his conflict, and when she was no more it drove him into actual insanity. She was, like his exaggerated belief in his own greatness, a necessary part of the fiction by which he lived.

So far no reference has been made to Poe's literary work because it seemed worth while before describing it to get some understanding of the inward life from which it sprang, but in closing this discussion of his sexual nature, one poem, written not long before his death, may be quoted for the light which it throws upon this nature. To read it even casually is to get the impression, so commonly produced by Poe's poetry, of a profound and despairing moodiness sometimes expressed in almost meaningless jargon or in rather tawdry melodrama, but to regard it a little more closely is to perceive an easily interpretable symbolism.

ULALUME

The skies they were ashen and sober;
    The leaves they were crisped and sere—
    The leaves they were withering and sere;
It was night in the lonesome October
    Of my most immemorial year;
It was hard by the dim lake of Auber,
    In the misty mid region of Weir—
It was down by the dank tarn of Auber,
    In the ghoul-haunted woodland of Weir.

Here once, through an alley Titanic,
    Of cypress, I roamed with my Soul—
    Of cypress, with Psyche, my Soul.
These were days when my heart was volcanic
    As the scoriac rivers that roll—
    As the lavas that restlessly roll
Their sulphurous currents down Yaanek
    In the ultimate climes of the pole—
That groan as they roll down Mount Yaanek
    In the realms of the boreal pole.

Our talk had been serious and sober,
    But our thoughts they were palsied and sere—
    Our memories were treacherous and sere—
For we knew not the month was October,
    And we marked not the night of the year—
    (Ah, night of all nights in the year!)
We noted not the dim lake of Auber—
    (Though once we had journeyed down here)—
Remembered not the dank tarn of Auber,
    Nor the ghoul-haunted woodland of Weir.

And now, as the night was senescent
 And star-dials pointed to morn—
 As the star-dials hinted of morn—
At the end of our path a liquescent
 And nebulous lustre was born,
Out of which a miraculous crescent
 Arose with a duplicate horn—
Astarte's bediamonded crescent
 Distinct with its duplicate horn.

And I said—"She is warmer than Dian:
 She rolls through an ether of sighs—
 She revels in a region of sighs:
She has seen that the tears are not dry on
 These cheeks, where the worm never dies
And has come past the stars of the Lion,
 To point us the path to the skies—
 To the Lethean peace of the skies—
Come up, in despite of the Lion,
 To shine on us with her bright eyes—
Come up through the lair of the Lion,
 With love in her luminous eyes."

But Psyche, uplifting her finger,
 Said—"Sadly this star I mistrust—
 Her pallor I strangely mistrust:—
Oh, hasten!—oh, let us not linger!
 Oh, fly!—let us fly!—for we must."
In terror she spoke, letting sink her
 Wings till they trailed in the dust—
In agony sobbed, letting sink her
 Plumes till they trailed in the dust—
 Till they sorrowfully trailed in the dust.

I replied—"This is nothing but dreaming:
 Let us on by this tremulous light!
 Let us bathe in this crystalline light!

Its Sibyllic splendor is beaming
    With Hope and in Beauty to-night:—
    See!—it flickers up the sky through the night!
Ah, we safely may trust to its gleaming,
    And be sure it will lead us aright—
We safely may trust to a gleaming
    That cannot but guide us aright,
    Since it flickers up to Heaven through the night."

Thus I pacified Psyche and kissed her;
    And tempted her out of her gloom—
    And conquered her scruples and gloom;
And we passed to the end of the vista,
    But were stopped by the door of a tomb—
    By the door of a legended tomb;
And I said—"What is written, sweet sister,
    On the door of this legended tomb?"
    She replied—"Ulalume—Ulalume—
    'Tis the vault of thy lost Ulalume!"

Then my heart it grew ashen and sober
    As the leaves that were crisped and sere—
    As the leaves that were withering and sere,
And I cried—"It was surely October
    On *this* very night of last year
    That I journeyed—I journeyed down here—
    That I brought a dread burden down here—
    On this night of all nights in the year,
    Ah, what demon has tempted me here?
Well I know, now, the dank tarn of Auber,
    This misty mid region of Weir—
Well I know, now, the dank tarn of Auber,
    This ghoul-haunted woodland of weir."

It has been suggested that this poem, with its description of hopeless hope, is merely a reflection of the poet's agony as he was compelled to watch the dying struggles of his wife who rallied only to sink again, but it is impossible to understand, if this be the case, why Diana and Astarte, never known to symbolize life and death, should play so important a rôle. Diana is, however, commonly known as the chaste goddess, and Astarte has symbolized in innumerable poems the love which is in part at least of the flesh. In the present poem it is she who tempts the poet and she who, in spite of the warning of his true goddess, leads him away only to bring him once more face to face with the tomb whose closed doors, so he now remembers, shut him forever from the possibility of further love.

Who, then, was this mysterious Ulalume or, as he had called her in more than one previous poem, this "lost Lenore"? It was not actually Virginia, for though she was dead when the particular poem in question was written, Poe had lamented the death of many a radiant maiden during the period when Virginia still lived, and Virginia was at most only a fleshly embodiment whose sexlessness enabled her to represent the lost one whose memory protected him against whoever was the "Astarte" of the moment. Were Ulalume and Lenore phantoms of that Miss Royster whom he loved as a youth in Richmond and to whom he returned after the death of Virginia; were they Mrs. Stanard whose hand he had kissed in childhood and who haunted him as the Helen of his poems; or were they rather the mother of dim subconscious memory who had, perhaps, reëmbodied herself in those other two women who held his fancy captive until he found in the unearthly Virginia some escape? To this question no final answer can be given. Psychiatrists may quarrel over the question of whether or not an inhibition such as his must actually arise from a previous experience and a consequent fixation or whether it may have some organic cause. But one thing is fairly certain. Poe could not love in the normal fashion and the reason lay, or at least seemed to him to lay, in the death of some woman upon whom his desire had irrevocably fixed itself. If we knew who lay behind the doors of that tomb in the ghoul-haunted woodland of Weir, we should know the answer to the greatest riddle of Poe's life.

IV

THE MISTY MID REGION OF WEIR

OCCASIONALLY, and especially when he was under the influence of drink, Poe would express himself in words or actions which seemed to come from the same diabolic sources which inspired his tales; but there was ordinarily nothing—except his air of profound melancholy—in either his manner or his way of life to suggest that he was other than a gentle and hardworking man of conventional opinions and regular habits. There was, especially, nothing about the existence which he began with his young bride in Richmond which was not pathetically modest and humdrum. A little later people began to remark that he was somewhat fonder of social and convivial life than a newly married gentleman should be, but there is nothing so commonplace and respectable as a boarding house, and Poe's newly acquired mother set up a boarding house in order that the young writer's modest salary (soon raised to eight hundred and fifty dollars a year) might be adequate.

With a certain insouciance such as always marked his requests for money, Poe, it seems, had borrowed one hundred dollars each from a relative and from Mr. Kennedy with which to rent a house, and now he began to live in it as the first of his mother-in-law's boarders. The people among whom he moved were almost eighteenth-century in their normal respectability, the magazine for which he wrote was a respectable provincial venture,

63

and the outward circumstances of his life, save for the mysterious presence of the strange child wife, were as lacking in romantic color as anything one can well imagine. From his surroundings he could draw nothing not bathed in the full light of the most commonplace day, and yet in the copy which he handed to the printer there was nothing which bore any relation to the life which he lived. His imagination was fed wholly from within, and from the boarding house issued a series of tales which were to furnish Europe with a new thrill. Fortunately for Poe his quality was not immediately recognized. People complained that he was unnecessarily terrific, and his staunchest friend, Mr. Kennedy, solemnly suggested that he try to write something after the manner of the French Vaudeville. But there was a tradition of melodrama and rather ghastly sentiment in the magazines of the time, and Poe was generally credited with an ingenious imitation of this fashion. Had his contemporaries suspected that he wrote as he did not because he wanted to but because he could write in no other way, that he was not playing with morbid horrors but mastered by them, the outcry against him would have been raised sooner than it was, and eminently healthy men like the Honorable Beverly Tucker would not have begun, as they did, to sing his praises. Soon enough they began to deprecate the sinister aspects of his character: but fortunately they did not recognize that his genius was no more than the power to express that character in perfect symbols. Even as it was, however, Poe had not long ceased to be the editor of the *Messenger* when its owner refused to print *The Fall of the House of Usher* because he doubted "whether the readers of the

64

Messenger have much relish for tales of the German school."

Most of the stories published in the *Messenger* had been written during the obscure Baltimore period, and it was during that period that Poe first discovered his genius. Three times previously he had appeared, though far from conspicuously, as a poet, for he had published three volumes, *Tamerlane and other Poems* (Boston 1827), *Al Aaraaf, Tamerlane and Minor Poems* (Baltimore 1829), and *Poems* (New York 1831); but all were, save for a few poems, distinctly prentice work. Critics as in duty bound often fancy that they see in many of them at least an adumbration of greatness, but the majority of them are highly imitative and nearly worthless. The young poet who wrote them was obviously already a victim of melancholy and pride, but either these emotions were still half unreal or he had not yet learned to express them in any individual manner. It was natural that a young man who felt, as Poe did, desperately isolated from the rest of mankind should find his model in the most popular poet of melodramatic isolation and so, though traces of Keats, Shelley, and Coleridge have been found in him, the dominant influence is obviously Byronic.

In the volume of 1827 he begins, for example, a poem with the lines

> Oh! that my young life were a lasting dream!
> My spirit not awaking, till the beam
> Of an eternity should bring the morrow.

and one may see in them, perhaps, an attempt to express that dissatisfaction with reality and that desire to es-

cape into the imaginary world which he created and
which, in spite of all its horror, obviously answered the
needs of his spirit in a way which the real world did not;
but this expression does not in any way differentiate
his longing from the conventional longing of the poet
for "dreams"; and the lines which follow definitely throw
the reader off the track by identifying the spirit of the
author with the melodrama of Byron:

> Yes! tho' that long dream were of hopeless sorrow,
> 'T were better than the cold reality
> Of waking life, to him whose heart must be,
> And hath been still, upon this lovely earth,
> A chaos of deep passion, from his birth.

Now the fact that to Poe, though his dream was a
dream "of hopeless sorrow," it was preferable to "cold
reality" is the center of his mystery; but it is here made
only incidental to a conventional theme, and it is lost in
the stereotyped emotions which surround it. When he
was not, in these earlier volumes, imitating Byron or
Coleridge he was imitating those gently sentimental magazine poets of whom L. E. Landon was the type and
writing poems like the well known one beginning "I saw
thee on thy bridal day," which deals, it is true, with a
characteristic theme—unconsummated love—but deals
with it in such a way that it seems to be only sentimental
melodrama without that touch of morbid sensuality which
gives the characteristic flavor to Poe's treatment of the
theme and which springs from the fact that to him such
frustration was not, because of his psychic abnormality,
pure pain. Upon the conscious level it was what it
would be to any normal person—a source of melancholy

distress; but unconsciously it was also the highest satisfaction attainable, because to him consummation was impossible and the nearest which he could approach to
voluptuousness was in the contemplation of a situation
in which the natural expression of desire is made impossible by outward circumstance instead of being inhibited,
as it always was with him, by psychic incapacity.

The poem quoted at the end of the preceding chapter
is a great poem because, if it is understood at all, it can
be understood only as a highly personal emotion; that
just referred to is entirely insignificant because, whatever the emotion from which it sprung, there is nothing
in the expression to distinguish it from conventional sentiment. To include it, as is sometimes done, among
Poe's best poems is simply to admire him (as is common
enough among his sentimental devotees) for qualities
which do not raise him much above his contemporary,
Mrs. Sigourney, and which would not have kept his
memory alive five years after his death.

The volume of 1829 contained two good poems—
Romance and *To Science*—and in the volume of 1831
appear *To Helen, Israfel, The City in the Sea,* and an
inferior version of one of his best pieces, *Lenore;* but it
was in prose that he first unmistakably revealed his
genius, and it was during the dark years in Baltimore
that he first discovered it. It was then, as we have said,
that he suffered his deepest humiliation, and it was then
that he was, for the first time, deprived of any external
support either from fame or from the hope of an aristocratic self-sufficiency. Hence he was for the first time
also compelled to find in fancy a satisfaction for the needs
of his spirit. "The realities of the world," he says of

the hero of *Berenice,* "affected me as visions, and visions only, while the wild ideas of the land of dreams became, in turn—not the material of my every-day existence— but in very deed that existence utterly and solely in itself."

This strange world of his imagination was the only one in which Poe could dwell, and he never left it once it had been found. The problem which he offers is the problem of discovering why this world, apparently so terrible, was the one in which his spirit could obtain the nearest possible approach to the peace which he sought, and in order to suggest a solution to the problem it is necessary first to describe that world and then to relate it to the aspects of his character which have been described.

The prize story *MS Found in a Bottle* was published in the *Baltimore Saturday Visiter* for October 12, 1833, and during the years 1835, 1836, 1837, and 1838 Poe published fifteen more tales, all except two of them in the *Messenger.* Superficially these tales represent a considerable variety, but there is not one which would not be recognized immediately by any reader as indubitably Poe's, and this means that they are, without exception, visions of his own peculiar world. What, we must ask, are the dominant characteristics of this world?

Over and over again—in connection with a tale, in an essay in literary criticism, and in his collection of scattered *pensées*—Poe quoted a sentence from Lord Verulam: "There is no exquisite beauty without some strangeness in the proportions," and the meaning which he read into it was not only the central thesis of his esthetic but also the law of his imagination. By strange-

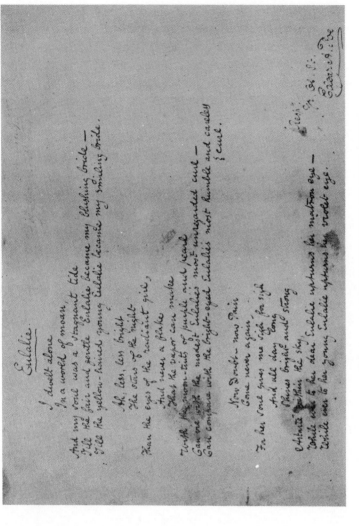

AUTOGRAPHED MANUSCRIPT OF "EULALIE"

ness he meant not merely novelty but positive abnormality; his world is essentially a world in which abnormality has become normal—and in which nothing ever looks or no one ever feels in a way which would not be either impossible or at least highly unusual in the universe which the undisturbed senses see and react to.

That world of physical nature which forms the background of his stories is either one cut off completely from the rest of the world or one in which all law is suspended. His people inhabit some world of Fay, wander in some hitherto undiscovered corner of earth which seems to lie in a dimension unknown to us, or, shut off from the rest of the world by the walls of some crumbling castle, they move in the midst of a *décor* which they have deliberately made as fantastically different from that of a normal dwelling as can possibly be imagined. Never feeling a normal emotion, they never see a normal sight.

No beam of sunlight falls upon any object; light emanating from fitfully burning braziers is stained through colored glasses before it is allowed to illuminate the velvet hangings which cover the walls; the senses, instead of being refreshed by pure air, are "oppressed by mingled and conflicting perfumes, reeking up from strange convolute censers together with multitudinous flaming and flickering tinges of emerald and violet fire"; and if we have, not an interior but an exterior, then the heavenly bodies unite with trees and stones to set a stage in which the deranged mind of the hero will find his own temperament reflected.

Nature herself becomes unnatural and, disregarding her fixed laws, plays strange tricks upon him. In the land to which Arthur Gordon Pym, for instance, wanders, the brooks flow with strangely dyed liquids, and in the sea upon which the ill-fated mariner who is the hero of Poe's first story drifted, the water, "unnaturally clear," permits the eye to travel many fathoms into its depths. Even the sun, the most sane of all natural phenomena, becomes an object of terror; rising only a few degrees above the horizon, it first shone "with a sickly yellow lustre emitting no decisive light," and then, "just before sinking within the turgid sea, its central fires suddenly went out, as if extinguished by some unaccountable power," so that "it was a dim, silver-like rim, alone, as it rushed down the unfathomable ocean." Poe was a poet, but a poet so unusual that not even nature had for him any charm unless it had some aspect of nightmare strangeness.

Even for their moments of revelry or their rarer moments of happiness his heroes deliberately choose—and this fact is of great significance—the most lugubrious possible surroundings, because for them as for their creator the idea of voluptuous pleasure cannot be dissociated from the idea of melancholy and horror. In the tale called *Shadow* some revellers gather to drink wine, but they gather round an ebony table and their chairman is a corpse:

"Over some flasks of the red Chian wine, within the walls of a noble hall, in a dim city called Ptolemais, we sat, at night, a company of seven. And to our chamber there was no entrance save by a lofty door of brass; and the door was fashioned by the artizan Corinnos, and, being of rare workmanship, was fastened from within. Black draperies, likewise, in the gloomy room, shut out from our view the moon, the lurid stars and the people-less streets—but the boding and the memory of Evil, they would not be so excluded. There were things around us and about of which I can render no distinct account —things material and spiritual—heaviness in the atmosphere—a sense of suffocation—anxiety—and, above all, that terrible state of existence which the nervous experience when the senses are keenly living and awake, and meanwhile the powers of thought lie dormant. A dead weight hung upon us. It hung upon our limbs— upon the household furniture—upon the goblets from which we drank; and all things were depressed, and borne down thereby—all things save only the flames of the seven iron lamps which illumined our revel. Uprearing themselves in tall slender lines of light, thus they remained burning all pallid and motionless, and in the mirror which their lustre formed upon the round table of ebony at which we sat, each of us there assembled beheld the pallor of his own countenance, and the unquiet glare in the downcast eyes of his companions. Yet we laughed and were merry in our proper way—which was hysterical; and sang the songs of Anacreon—which are madness; and drank deeply—although the purple wine reminded us of blood. For there was yet another tenant of our chamber in the person of young Zoilus. Dead, at full length he lay, enshrouded;—the genius and the demon of the scene. Alas! he bore no portion in our mirth, save that his countenance, distorted with the plague, and his eyes in which Death had but half extinguished the fire of the pestilence, seemed to take such interest in our merriment as the dead may haply take in the merriment of those who are to die. But though I, Oinos, felt that the eyes of the departed were upon me, still I forced myself not to perceive the bitterness of their expression, and, gazing down steadily into the depths of the ebony mirror, sang with a loud and sonorous voice the songs of the son of Teios."

Such is the convivial debauchery of the characters of Poe, and even stranger is their idea of the surroundings amid which they may suitably consummate their nuptial happiness:

"I have said that I minutely remember the details of the chamber—yet I am sadly forgetful on topics of deep moment—and here there is no system, no keeping, in the fantastic display, to take hold of the memory. The room lay in a high turret of the castellated abby, was pentagonal in shape, and of capacious size. Occupying the whole southern face of the pentagon was the sole window—an immense sheet of unbroken glass from Venice—a single pane, and tinted of a leaden hue so that the rays of either the sun or moon, passing through it, fell with a ghastly lustre on the objects within. Over the upper portion of this huge window, extended the trellis-work of an aged vine, which clambered up the massy walls of the turret. The ceiling, of gloomy looking oak, was excessively lofty, vaulted, and elaborately fretted with the wildest and most grotesque specimens of a semi-Gothic, semi-Druidical device. From out the most central recess of this melancholy vaulting, depended, by a single chain of gold with long links, a huge censer of the same metal, Saracenic in pattern, and with many perforations so contrived that there writhed in and out of them as if endued with a serpent vitality, a continual succession of parti-colored fires.

"Some few ottomans and gold candelabra of Eastern

figure, were in various stations about—and there was the couch, too—the bridal couch—of an Indian model, and low, and sculptured of solid ebony, with a pall-like canopy above. In each of the angles of the chamber stood on end a gigantic sarcophagous of black granite from the tombs of the kings over against Luxor, with their aged lids full of immemorial sculpture. But in the draping of the apartment lay, alas! the chief phantasy of all. The lofty walls, gigantic in height—even unproportionally so—were hung from summit to foot, in vast folds, with a heavy and massive looking tapestry of a material which was found alike as a carpet on the floor, as a covering for the ottomans and the ebony bed, as a canopy for the bed, and as the gorgeous volutes of the curtains which partially shaded the window. The material was the richest cloth of gold. It was spotted all over, at irregular intervals, with arabesque figures, about a foot in diameter and wrought upon the cloth in patterns of the most jetty black. But these figures partook of the true character of the arabesque only when regarded from a single point of view. By a contrivance now quite common and indeed traceable to a very remote period of antiquity, they were made changeable in aspect. To one entering the room, they bore the appearance of simple monstrosities; but upon further advance, this appearance gradually departed; and step by step as the visitor moved his station in the chamber, he saw himself surrounded by an endless succession of ghastly forms which belong to the superstition of the Norman, or arise in the guilty slumbers of the monk. The phantasmagoric effect was vastly heightened by the artificial introduction of a strong continual current of wind behind the draperies—giving a hideous and uneasy animation to the whole.

"In halls such as these—in a bridal chamber such as this, I passed—with the Lady of Tremaine, the unhallowed hours of the first month of our marriage—passed them with but little disquietude."

The minds and temperaments of the characters of the stories are such as would conceive these exploits and enjoy these pleasures. The men have usually no name, no family, and no history. "Of my country and of my family," begins Poe's first story, "I have little to say. Ill usage and length of years have driven me from the one and estranged me from the other." Yet even this hero is less mysterious than most, for the tellers of the tales are generally vaguer still and seem to have all but forgotten any tie which might once have united them to the rest of mankind for they usually belong to a degenerate aristocracy which is about to extinguish itself with them and they inhabit crumbling castles which the world seems to have forgotten. "My baptismal name," says one, "is Egæus; that of my family I will not mention. Yet there are no towers in the land more time-honored than my gloomy, gray, hereditary halls"; and he is completely typical. None has a single relationship or a single interest to connect him in any way with his fellow creatures, and each is plunged in the same abstruse studies which take him further away from humanity. Upon each has fallen some strange paralysis which condemns him to pass his life in a dream from which he cannot waken, and to feel no passions except those which are fantastic and unreasonable. These men love but it is with a strange love; they feel, but their feelings have no

74

rational basis, and it is always a "feeling for which I have no name—a sensation which will admit of no analysis, to which the lessons of bygone times are inadequate, and for which I fear futurity itself will offer no key." Or as another says, "The fires were not of Eros, and bitter and tormenting to my spirit was the gradual conviction that I could in no manner define their unusual meaning, or regulate their vague intensity, yet we met; and fate bound us together at the altar; and I never spoke of passion, nor thought of love. She, however, shunned society, and, attaching herself to me alone, rendered me happy."

Nor are the objects of these passions less strange than those who feel them or than the passions themselves. The heroines, like the heroes, bear no names of this earth; they are called Berenice, Morella, Ligeia, or Ulalume, and they, too, have descended from families too shadowy or too terrible to have recorded histories. They do not come into the lives of the heroes, they simply *are*. Of one it is said: "I cannot, for my soul, remember how, when, or even precisely where, I first became acquainted with the lady Ligeia," and what is said of her is equally true of the others because each is the phantom projection of the hero's need, born of no parents except his conflict of desires and encountered nowhere except in one of those fantasies to which the needs give rise. Each, too, is, like the heroes, strangely learned in some half specified and forbidden learning which, if it does not "actually serve to irritate the disorder" from which both suffer, nevertheless partakes in "the imaginative and inconsequential nature of the characteristic qualities of the disorder itself"; and each, beautiful with a strange, pale,

unearthly beauty, is wasting away from an unknown
malady. Disease, a fatal disease, fell like the simoon
upon the frame of Berenice, "and even while I gazed upon
her, the spirit of change swept over her, pervading her
mind, her habits, and her character, and, in a manner
most subtle and terrible, disturbing even the identity of
her person! Alas! the destroyer came and went, and
the victim—where was she? I knew her not or knew
her no longer as Berenice." Morella "pined away daily.
In time, the crimson spot settled steadily upon the cheek,
the blue veins upon the pale forehead became prominent;
but the fragile spirit clung to its tenement of clay for
many days—for many weeks and irksome months—until
my tortured nerves obtained the mastery over my mind
and I grew furious through delay. . . . But one autum-
nal evening, when the winds lay still in heaven Morella
called me to her bedside—'It is the day of days,' she said,
as I approached; 'a day of all other days either to live
or die. It is a fair day for the sons of earth and life—
ay, more fair for the daughters of heaven and death!—
I am dying, yet shall I live.' " "Ligeia grew ill. The
wild eyes blazed with a too—too glorious effulgence;
the pale fingers became of the transparent waxen hue
of the grave, and the blue veins upon the lofty forehead
swelled and sank impetuously with the tides of the most
gentle emotion. . . . Words are impotent to convey any
just idea of the fierceness of the resistance with which she
wrestled with the Shadow. I groaned with anguish at
the pitiable spectacle. . . . And as she breathed her last
sighs, there came mingled with them a low murmur from
her lips. I bent to them my ear and distinguished,
again, the concluding words of the passage in Glanvil—

'Man doth not yield him to the angels, nor unto death utterly, save only through the weakness of his feeble will!' "

In the eleven years of life which were left to him after the publication of the story from which this last quotation is taken Poe wrote many more tales and he invented a new genre—the tale of ratiocination—but again and again he returned to the material which we have just described, and in all of his best stories the same features reappear. *The Masque of the Red Death* is merely the most perfect description of that fantastic *décor* which he had again and again imagined; *The Fall of the House of Usher* is merely an even more elaborate arrangement of the stock scenes, stock characters, and stock situations, for it too is the story of a learned madman inhabiting a decaying and fantastic castle and loving an unearthly woman who like Morella and Ligeia wastes away of a strange disease and rises in a brief resurrection from the tomb to which he has conducted her. Whenever Poe turned to his imagination for material the same vision reappeared to him, unbidden, like a recurrent dream or, more exactly, like the recurrent fantasy which constitutes the obsession of those on the brink of certain kinds of madness.

Poe himself rationalized his practice, but it is obvious that somehow his imagination mastered him and that the formation of his favorite themes was one from which he could not escape. His stories are too full of life and in detail too richly varied to be mechanical copies of one another, but they are in essence too similar not to be expressions of a mastering interest. Dreamlike in their power to make fantastic unrealities seem real, they are dreams in essence, experiences, that is to say, which satisfy in some way the desires of the dreamer. That these desires were abnormal and that they were ones not likely to be wholly realized in waking life, both the character of the dreams and the character of the dreamer would of themselves suggest; and to consider a little more closely certain aspects of the stories is to connect them even more intimately with the character of their creator.

By even the most casual of lay observers the stories would be described as "morbid" and "neurotic" because they represent a desperate flight from all reality and because the world into which the author escapes is one which would seem to the ordinary man not more but less satisfying than actuality. To go further and to catalogue the incidents, characters, and thoughts is to perceive that they constitute almost the complete repertory of neurotic delights from the simple sadism of such mature stories as *Hop Frog, The Cask of Amontillado*, and *The Pit and the Pendulum* to the most elaborate of perversities like that described in *Berenice*, where the hero mutilates the object of his ambivalent passion, composed half of love and half of hate, in order to extract from her mouth the teeth upon which his desires have become fixed, or like that which forms the basis of *The Black Cat*, in which the hero is seized by an unreasonable and irresistible desire to torture the cat which has been his pet.

It is, moreover, worth observing that in the majority of cases the emotions and actions of the characters are apparently unmotivated. They fear they know not what, and they are oppressed with a sense of guilt which is either frankly baseless or the result of some deed which the author, unable to imagine, tells us is too terrible to be mentioned. Nameless night terrors seize them, they spend whole hours in states of absolute unconsciousness, and they commit murders not for revenge but merely because of a mastering obsession or an immovable fixation which has attached itself to a black cat, the eye of a harmless old man, or the teeth of a beautiful woman. "Presently," says one, "I heard a slight groan, and I knew it was the groan of mortal terror. . . . I knew the sound well. Many a night, just at midnight, when all the world slept, it has welled up from my own bosom, deepening, with its dreadful echo, the terrors that distracted me." "Let me call myself, for the present, William Wilson," says another. "The fair page now lying before me need not be sullied with my real appellation. This has been already too much an object for the scorn—for the horror—for the detestation of my race. To the uttermost regions of the globe have not the indignant winds bruited its unparalleled infamy? Oh, outcast of outcasts most abandoned! to the earth art thou not forever dead? to its honors, to its flowers, to its golden aspirations? and a cloud, dense, dismal, and limitless, does it not hang eternally between thy hopes and heaven? I would not, if I could, here or to-day, embody a record of my later years of unspeakable misery, and unpardonable crime."

Certain gruesome subjects, especially those connected with premature burial and temporary resurrection from the dead, occupy them constantly, and it is objects or visions of terror which give them the ambiguous pleasure which alone they can experience. They have what Poe himself describes as "the human taste for self-torture" and Arthur Gordon Pym speaks for the majority when he

says, referring to his youthful dreams of adventure at sea: "For the bright side of the painting I had a limited sympathy. My visions were of shipwreck and famine; of death or captivity among barbarian hordes; of a lifetime dragged out in sorrow and tears, upon some gray and desolate rock, in an ocean unapproachable and unknown. Such visions or desires—for they amounted to desires—are common, I have since been assured, to the whole numerous race of the melancholy among men— at the time of which I speak I regarded them only as prophetic glimpses of a destiny which I felt myself in a measure bound to fulfill."

Easy as it is to perceive in all these stories the fulfillment of a morbid wish, it is not easy to discover the source from which these wishes arise, nor is Poe himself able to throw much light upon the question with which it is obvious his own highly developed faculty of rationalization was much occupied. "The dreamer," so he makes the hero of *Berenice* say, in describing the mental malady which possessed him, "being interested by an object usually *not* frivolous, imperceptibly loses sight of this object in a wilderness of deductions and suggestions issuing therefrom, until, at the conclusion of a day dream *often replete with luxury*, he finds the *incitamentum* or first cause of his musings entirely vanished and forgotten"; and this is probably a fairly accurate account of the process by which one of his fantasies took possession of him. But it does nothing to account for their cause. Similarly, when he said again in the essay-tale *Premature Burial*, "we thrill, for example, with the most intense of 'pleasurable pain,' over the accounts of the Passage of Beresina, of the Earthquake at Lisbon, of the Plague at London, of the Massacre of St. Bartholomew, or of the stifling of the hundred and twenty-three prisoners in the Black Hole at Calcutta," he was able to do no more than state a fact true to a slight extent of all, but by no means the simple law of human nature which it appeared to him to be.

Nor could he ever get much further than this in his analysis; and finally, in *The Imp of the Perverse*, he was compelled to fall back upon the assumption of an as yet unrecognized but fundamental human trait called perversity. "Induction, *à posteriori*, would," says the hero of this tale, in explaining his irresistible impulse to confess a murder, "have brought phrenology to admit, as an innate and primitive principle of human action, a paradoxical something, which we may call *perverseness* for want of a more characteristic term. In the sense I intend, it is, in fact, a *mobile* without motive, a motive not *motivirt*. Through its promptings we act without comprehensible object; or, if this shall be understood as a contradiction in terms, we may so far modify the proposition as to say, that through its promptings we act, for the reason that we should *not*. In theory, no reason can be more unreasonable; but in fact, there is none more strong. With certain minds, under certain conditions, it becomes absolutely irresistible. I am not more certain that I breathe than that the assurance of the wrong or error of any action is often the one unconquerable *force* which impels us to its prosecution. Nor will this overwhelming tendency to do wrong for the wrong's sake, admit of analysis, or resolution into ulterior elements. It is a radical, a primitive impulse-elementary."

Stripped of its metaphysical and pseudo-scientific jargon this passage remains a confession of Poe's complete inability to account for the apparent perverseness of his own tastes, thoughts, and actions, and of the fact that he was forced to explain them on the basis of a natural human appetite. But of this as of his other explanations it can only be said that though it contains a certain germ of truth—for all men are occasionally perverse in their tastes, as the common liking for Poe's stories will, for example, prove—it does not nevertheless explain why that which is a fugitive impulse in others was with him the dominant passion or why perversity was the law of his being.

Perhaps the key to his morbidity may be found in a negative characteristic of his writings which has not yet been mentioned—namely, their complete sexlessness. Of Poe it has often been said with entire truth that whatever objections might be made to the tone of his stories it could not be denied that they are without a single exception "pure," and that though they may deal with every other horror and corruption known to man they are free from every taint of sexual indelicacy. He could pile horror upon horror, he could revel in blood and putrefaction to such an extent that some of his inferior stories like *King Pest*, for example, almost deserve the denunciation which Stevenson in an early review gave them when he said that the person who wrote them had ceased to be human; but of any sensuality normal enough to be recognized as such by the reader unfamiliar with morbid psychology there is not a trace. The hero of *Berenice*, who describes at some length how his love for the heroine turned gradually and without cause into such an irra-

tional hate that he murdered her in a trance which came
upon him, would be diagnosed by any psychiatrist, no
matter to what school he might belong, as a sexual per-
vert of some kind.   And yet, however full the tales may
be of sex disguised and perverted, there is never from
the first to the last any recognition of the existence of
normal amorousness, which is indeed excluded in exactly
the same way that all the other interests of normal life
are excluded.

Poe was, it should be remembered, in his own character
morbidly pure. For women he had all his life an intense regard which degenerated in his latter days into a
disgustingly weak dependence upon them, and he tended
strongly toward that overvaluation of the opposite sex
which is common among even those neurotics who are intensely jealous, as he himself was, of any distinction recognized in members of their own sex; but he was not,
in the ordinary sense, a lover.   Speaking of women he
writes in *The Poetic Principle:* "No nobler *theme* ever
engaged the pen of a poet.   It is the soul elevating idea,
that no man can consider himself entitled to complain
of Fate while, in his adversity, he still retains the un-
wavering love of women. . . . He feels it [true poetry]
in the beauty of woman—in the grace of her step—in the
lustre of her eye—in the melody of her voice—in her
soft laughter—in her sigh—in the harmony of the rus-
tling of her robes. He deeply feels it in her winning
endearments—in her burning enthusiasms—in her gentle
charities—in her meek and devotional endurances—but
above all—ah; far above all—he kneels to it—he wor-
ships it in the faith, in the purity, in the strength, in

83

the altogether divine majesty of her *love.*" Yet he was, in the words of one (Wilmer) who knew him well, "of all the men I ever knew—the most *passionless.*"

His early love affairs appear to have been of the most romantically Platonic sort. In discussing the proper subject of poetry he explicitly excludes passion in spite of the fact that it is generally considered the most usual of poetic themes; and in writing of others, especially of female poets, one of the phrases which comes most often to his pen is "passionate purity." It is, also, perhaps, not without significance that he thought one of the most original of American long poems to be *The Sinless Child,* or that he should have written the following sentence remarkable for the coupling of the last adjective with its noun: "The boyish poet love is indisputably the one of the human sentiments which most nearly realizes our dreams of the chastened voluptuousness of love."

The sexlessness of his work has, of course, often been noted, and it has generally been cited as an extenuation of the somewhat unhealthy character of a general tendency. Thus, as far back as 1863, James Hannay wrote in an English edition of the poems: "With all this passion for the Beautiful, no poet was ever less voluptuous. He never profaned his genius whatever else he profaned. . . . A sound of music—rising as from an unseen Ariel brings in a most pure and lovely figure,— sad usually; so delicate and so dreamy are these conceptions, that, indeed, they hint only of some transparent beauty—some region where passion has no place"; and in a similar vein another remarked: "The female creations of his fancy are all either statues or angels." Yet no one seems to have cared to express the thought which

must have occurred to most of his modern readers or to
indicate that this extenuating circumstance is probably
the cause of the thing extenuated. Purity as conscious
of itself as his was is closely akin to pruriency, and both
melancholia and sadism are frequently traceable to sexual obsessions.

Moreover, if we compare the typical stories already
described with the story of Poe's own life it is impossible
not to be struck with the parallel which they afford. The
typical hero, oppressed with a strange melancholy and
seeking relief in fantastic studies and speculations, is
plainly Poe himself. The heroines with the unearthly
beauty and the unhealthy purity which seem to set them
apart from the women of flesh and blood are not exactly
Virginia, but they are the phantoms to whom she, with
her morbid fragility and child-like mind, seemed better
to correspond than any other woman whom Poe had ever
seen. And, most important of all, both she and they
carried about them no suggestion of physical passion
but could be loved by one to whom the whole idea of
physical union was utterly repulsive. They are the ideal
of morbidly sexless beauty.

Thus if we compare the most striking action of Poe's
life with his most characteristic stories, the two seem to
spring from the same impulse, the one representing his
attempt to adjust himself to actuality and the other his
attempt to create, after the manner of neurotics, an imaginary world to fit the needs of his mind. Of all the
stories which deal with the relations between a man and
woman only two indicate even by implication the possibility of normal union, and in both the result of this
union is wholly evil. Something unearthly in the woman

seems to stand between her and the hero, and death soon comes to remove her, leaving him safe to dream over merely the idea of a woman instead of a woman herself.

In real life nothing stood between Poe and a realization of his infirmity except the youth, artificially prolonged by disease and mental simplicity, of his wife; but in his darkly voluptuous dreams death comes to rescue him definitely from the torturing conflict between desire and repugnance and to present him the situation which contains for him the acme of voluptuousness—one, that is to say, in which he can contemplate woman without realizing that it is not Youth or Death or Purity or Disease but only himself which stands between him and the possibility of normally consummated passion.

The adjustment of the neurotic is, like the analagous adjustment of the drunkard and the dope fiend, notoriously unsatisfactory and incomplete. It dulls without wholly obliterating the torture of conflicting desires. But just as the drunkard, though he cannot be said to be happy, prefers intoxication as something more tolerable than sobriety, so the neurotic prefers his fantasies to the actuality from which they give an escape, since, even though they be, as they usually are, tinged with horror, they furnish him satisfactions which his conscious mind may not be able to recognize. So it was with Poe. That sense of melancholy, foreboding, and horror which, even though its exact meaning is disputed, is generally recognized as the usual accompaniment of deeply inhibited sexual desires, made his life one long misery, and a similar cloud of horror hung over his stories. Perverse fancies of a usually sadistic character flitted through his mind accompanied by a sickening revulsion against their horror, and these two found a place in his tales alongside all manner of nightmare fears. And yet, taken as a whole, the world which he created was one which had, like his drunkenness, its origin in his need, and it furnished him a certain ambiguous satisfaction, as the persistence with which he dwelt in it will prove. In it he was able both to realize what was for him perfect love and also to indulge the sadistic perversities to which his malady gave rise. When he lived in imagination the lives of his heroes, escaped with them into strange worlds and luxuriated with them over the memory of strange departed maidens, he was living a life more satisfactory than that of the Richmond boarding house and creating a fantasy of himself nearer to his neurotic ideal than the underpaid editor that he actually was. And, by a triumph of that rationalizing faculty which he had to so marvelous a degree, he succeeded in translating an individual idiosyncracy into an aesthetic principle; for the most poetic of all ideas is, so he declared, the death of a beautiful woman, although he did not ever realize why this was peculiarly true for him.

Nor does it seem to be too fanciful to suggest one other parallel. These charming maidens whom death takes away will not rest in their graves but struggle with an indomitable will against dissolution. Sometimes they break forth, like the Lady Madeline, from their tombs, or again, like Ligeia, they take possession of the body of another. Thus, like the erotic imagination which gave them birth, they never really die but rise to plague their victim even at the moment when he thinks that he is done with them forever.

V

"WHY *WILL* YOU SAY THAT I AM MAD?"

FROM the very beginning of his journalistic career Poe achieved a sort of fame which was not convertible into prosperity but which was nevertheless highly congenial to him because it was dark, mysterious, and a little fearsome. Under his control the circulation of the *Messenger*, which had been begun by a practical printer of no particular culture, leaped from seven hundred to five thousand and became a journal of major importance in the literary world of America; but Poe's reputation was of an ambiguous sort, based partly upon stories which forced an unwilling and somewhat amazed admiration, partly upon a series of slashing book reviews which made fearlessness and impartiality an excuse for scornful denunciation descending sometimes to billingsgate. There will be occasion in discussing the intrinsic value of Poe's literary work to indicate the great importance of this criticism as well as the great importance of his creative writings, but for the understanding of his personality and career it is necessary to stress the ferocious and reckless egotism which inspired him.

"In summing up an opinion of 'Paul Ulric,'" he wrote in a typical early review selected at random, "it is by no means our intention to mince matters at all. The book is despicable in every respect. Such are the works which bring daily discredit upon our national literature. We have no right to complain of being laughed at abroad

when so villainous a compound, as the thing we now hold
in our hand, of incongruous folly, plagiarism, immoral-
ity, inanity, and bombast, can command at any moment
both a puff and a publisher.   To Mr. Mattson himself
we have only one word to say before throwing his book
into the fire.   Dress· it up, good sir, for the nursery."
Such was his habitual manner, and though no doubt the
book in question deserved all that it got, Poe assumed,
it will be remembered, a similar manner in his contro-
versies with established men, and from the beginning
he was obviously determined to make no bid for an inclusion in the kindly circle composed of such men as Longfellow and Lowell, who constituted the literary world of
America.   The young critic as well as the young ro-
mancer was one who would inspire fear but not love,
and would get no more admiration than he could wring
half unwillingly from the contemporaries whom he despised.

Stung by the humiliation born of some sense of inferiority connected with the inhibition of his passions, and
enormously irritated by the sufferings which he had
undergone as a ward of Mr. Allan, Poe sought in gratified pride a balm for his feelings; but this balm was
most soothing when recognition was not begged but demanded.   That he was a misanthrope we have the evidence not only of his stories and the history of his
innumerable quarrels with almost everyone whom he knew
but also a recorded statement of his concerning the
"multitude, every individual of which I despise" as well
as the statement of one of his defenders, Mrs. E. Oakes
Smith, who wrote: "The real contempt which Poe felt
for his contemporaries came out at once under the in-

fluence of the wine-cup and he ridiculed, satirised, imitated and abused them right and left without mercy." When we couple this with the almost insane thirst for notoriety which he expressed in the exclamation: "I love fame—I dote on it—I idolize it—I would drink to the very dregs the glorious intoxication; I would have incense arise in my honor from every hill and hamlet, from every town and city on this earth; Fame! Glory!—they are life-giving breath, and living blood; no man lives, unless he is famous; how bitterly I belied my nature and my aspirations, when I said I did not desire fame and that I despised it!" we cannot possibly escape the conclusion that the ultimate felicity for which Poe strove was the double sense of superiority which comes from distributing contempt and receiving adulation. Griswold, however much he may have been moved by malice and however incompletely and distorted his famous article on Poe may have been, was not wholly wrong when he wrote: "He had, to a morbid excess, that desire to rise which is vulgarly called ambition, but no wish for the esteem or the love of his species; only the hard wish to succeed—not shine, nor serve—succeed, that he might have the right to despise a world which galled his self-conceit."

It is, so the psychopathologists tell us, the central characteristic of the neurotic to live by a fiction, and his vagaries are attempts, direct or indirect, to realize that fiction. Beginning with some sense of inferiority, he seeks methods of self-reassurance or self-glorification and, in fully developed cases, he invents a legend of himself which it is his constant effort to realize both in his fantasies and, as completely as possible, in his life. So it was with Poe. The description which Griswold gave of him and from which, after quoting it in extension in the first chapter, we have just made a brief citation, was a fairly accurate description of the legend which Poe sought to build, however much it may have left out of account the amiable features of his natural character. Just as his marriage and the recurrent central situation of so many stories represent the two faces, one actual the other imaginative, of his attempt to make an adjustment to existence, so the part which he played in life was the attempt to act out the rôle which he imagined for himself when he created the various dark heroes of his tales; and the ferocity of his criticism played its part in building the legend of himself as a man cut off from the majority of mankind by great learning, strange passions, and dark destiny, yet not inferior but superior to those with whom he made no part.

With the rest of mankind he could not compete in any ordinary field. His dream that he might play the rôle of Virginia aristocrat had long passed, and when he turned to authorship it was evident that the fancies which thronged his brain were not of the sort to win for him indiscriminate popularity. Moreover, both his poverty and his intemperance made it impossible for him to think of playing the rôle of popular lion; but all of these things did, on the contrary, point to the fact that whatever eminence he was to obtain it must of necessity be a dark eminence, and it was accordingly that for which he strove. Plunging into the task of reviewing which his editorial position gave to him, he began a career of reckless slashing which was undoubtedly exactly what the America of the moment needed, but which, it is impossible not to suspect, was also extremely congenial to the young reviewer who could thus at once make himself feared and to a certain extent realize his vision of himself as a man of power outside the circle of ordinary society. The reputation which he gained as a daringly caustic critic was the first step in the development of the legend which rapidly developed new features, the most important of which was the attribution to the central character of great and mysterious learning coupled with an inhuman capacity for pure abstract reason.

It is impossible to say how far back one should go in searching for the genesis of Poe's guiding fiction, but there is in an incident reported of his childhood which seems to indicate a mental process so strikingly similar to that from which many of his feats and pretenses sprang as to suggest that even as a boy he had begun to seek distinction in the manner characteristic of his maturity. "I remember," says a certain John T. L. Preston who was a fellow pupil of Poe's at a school near Richmond, "that he would allow the strongest boy in the school to strike him with full force in the chest. He taught me the secret, and I imitated him after my measure. It was to inflate the lungs to the uttermost, and at the moment of receiving the blow to exhale the air. It looked surprising, and was, indeed, a little rough; but with a good breast-bone, and some resolution it was not difficult to stand it." Now it would be absurd to insist too strongly upon the importance of this little incident, but the technic which it reveals—that of achieving a superiority by the exhibition of apparently unnatural powers based upon esoteric knowledge—is exactly that which Poe, with his parade of fictitious learning and his delight in amazing people with the exhibition of unusual powers, constantly practiced. The tale *A Descent into the Maelström*, with its story of a man saved by his peculiar knowledge of the properties of a cylinder in a vortex, is, to take a single example, an unusually close parallel, since it is an imaginary triumph of exactly the sort which Poe had actually achieved as a boy.

Certain it is that by the time he had written his first stories the tendency to pretend to strange knowledge was already evident. It will be remembered that at his first meeting with the judges of the *Visiter* contest he spoke of a story which he was writing concerning a voyage to the moon, and that he "at once went into a somewhat learned disquisition upon the laws of gravity, the height of the earth atmosphere, and the capacities of balloons." Now Poe's actual knowledge of science as of all other subjects was extremely meager, but he always acted as though he knew a great deal, and his various pseudo-scientific tales give the impression that he was thoroughly conversant with the laws of nature as well as with the most abstruse of philosophical speculations in spite of the fact that he never gave proof of any but the most smattering and inaccurate knowledge of any of the subjects upon which he spoke so glibly.

Of his philosophico-scientific scheme of the universe, *Eureka*, he said that the ground covered by Laplace compares with that covered by himself as a bubble compares the ocean on which it floats; and he probably himself believed in his science in spite of the fact that it is greatly erroneous in many of its fundamental assumptions—wrong not only in such points as the statement, which violates Newtonian principles, concerning the manner in which the planets rotate in elliptical orbits but in such easily ascertainable data as the density of the planets. And upon literary subjects he was, so far as knowledge was concerned, only less at sea than where science was concerned, for, to give an example, he could discuss the defects of the Greek dramatists and then so far betray his ignorance as to attribute *Oedipus at Colonos* to Aeschylus.

The strange and profound learning which he constantly attributes to his typical heroes is the same which he longed to have attributed to himself, in spite of the fact that he knew too little to be able to speak of their knowledge except in the most general terms—which failed to specify, save very vaguely, even the subjects in which they were learned. Real learning interested him as little as anything else real, but the idea of learning, with the sense of power which it bestows, was absolutely necessary to his support. Of the love of truth for its own sake as the scholar or the scientist knows it he knew nothing, and he made no systematic effort to learn anything except that which could be shown off; but he needed imperatively the fame which knowledge sometimes brings and the sense of superiority which those who do not have it imagine that it bestows. Thus he did not actually care to know, but was content if he could make it seem to others and to his own imagination that he did, and like all whose interest in science or philosophy is of this emotional sort he hankered constantly after those mysterious and easy short cuts to knowledge afforded by the various pseudo-sciences. Whatever gave vague promise of startling results without requiring any

EDGAR ALLAN POE

From an engraving of a painting by A. C. Smith

real study of complicated facts appealed to him immediately. References to mesmerism, character reading, and phrenology sprinkle his pages. And the latter subject he took with particular seriousness, returning to it again and again and discussing its flimsy hypotheses with a great show of scientific earnestness since it presented a very fruitful field for one who would appear to speak authoritatively upon a profound subject. When he discussed it he seemed learned, he felt learned, and he asked no more.

To say with Andrew Lang that Poe had a scholar's taste without a scholar's training is to forget that he lacked absolutely the humility which is a necessary part of the scholar's temperament and that his pretentiousness was enough, taken merely by itself, to suggest much more easily the perfect charlatan. Indeed the effort which he made to maintain to himself and others the phase of his guiding fiction here under discussion sometimes led him beyond the bounds of common honesty. To the *New York Review* for October 1827 he contributes a review of Stephens's *Travels in Arabia Petræa* in which he goes through the motions of learned commentary and discusses at considerable length the geographical and the theological aspects of the work, entering among other things into a very pretentious discussion of the appropriate translation of a Hebrew phrase concerning which his knowledge was absolutely nil. The review as a whole is carefully put together from material taken from two sources—the book itself and Keith's work on prophecy—while the Hebrew learning was supplied, as we have a letter in answer to Poe's request to prove, by Professor Charles Anthon. Nor

was this duplicity of Poe's the result of a merely
temporary aberration, for he seems to have been unusually proud of the article, and he reprinted his scrap
of borrowed learning at every opportunity, using it for
example in the collection of miscellaneous scraps known
as *Marginalia* which he published in the form of a
scholar's note-book jottings, but giving it as his own.
In another miscellany called *Pinikidia* he steals some of
his choicest bits from the elder Disraeli's collections, and
then in one of those ecstasies of mendacity into which
the faker sometimes falls he remarks satirically that
pretenders to erudition have been in the habit of stealing
from the *Curiosities of Literature, Literary Character*
and the *Calamities of Authors*—when this is exactly
what he is doing himself.

His citations from other than contemporary books
are almost always second-hand, and he often betrays the
fact although he never confesses it. Professor Wood-
berry points out, for example, that the quotation:
"And the angel Israfel, who has the sweetest voice of
all God's creatures," for example, which is prefixed to
Poe's poem *Israfel* and attributed to the Koran is not in
the Koran at all but in Sale's *Preliminary Discourse*,
which is quoted in an explanatory note to Tom Moore's
Lalla Rookh, from which Poe took it. Incidentally, and
in order to illustrate further the extent to which he had
"the instincts of a scholar," it may be added that later
he deliberately and without explanation amended this by
the addition of the phrase "whose heart strings are a
lute," which is found neither in Moore, Sale, nor the
Koran, but which may (though Woodberry does not notice this fact) have been suggested by the quotation from

Béranger used at the beginning of *The Fall of the House of Usher:*

> Son cœur est un luth suspendu;
> Sitôt qu'on le touche il résonne.

If one were to judge Poe by ordinary standards it would be necessary in view of such facts as those just recorded and of his persistent mendacity in regard to the events of his own life to set him down as a charlatan and a liar, but it is not, I think, necessary to pass a judgment so harsh. Truth and fiction were with him inextricably mingled, and imagination, being the result of an unconscious effort at psychic adjustment, outside his control. Sometimes it was so vivid as to constitute an actual hallucination, but being afterwards recognized as such it was written down as a story; at other times his wish to have done a certain thing or to have a certain power was so great that he could hardly distinguish the desire from the fact, and he pretended so passionately as almost to convince himself. We do not call a starving man who steals bread a thief, and there is no reason to call Poe a liar. The compensating sense of superiority he had to have; it was necessary for him if he was to maintain even the poor mental equilibrium which was his; and there was no choice for him save that between pretense and insanity.

Doubtless that intense love of mystification which led him to perpetrate hoaxes of one kind or another was the result of a somewhat similar desire to call attention to himself, and he seems to have taken great delight in the fact that his story of the mesmerization of a corpse (*The Facts in the Case of M. Valdemar*) was printed in

England as a genuine scientific report; but there is another aspect of his mind which calls for some explanation—the fact that puzzles of all sorts had a great fascination for him and that he seems in sober fact to have been extremely good at them. Not only might this seem at first sight somewhat strange in view of his unbalanced intellect, but it is paralleled by the fact that his best fiction falls definitely into two classes, the one consisting of tales so fantastic and so utterly irrational as to be vivid nightmares, and the other consisting of the tales called ratiocinative and depending upon pure logic which might seem to be the product of a mind completely devoid of imagination in the ordinary sense. The two classes have only one thing in common—a complete absence of human interest which results from the fact that they contain no observations of real character or manners and touch normal experience at no point; and in this similarity may be seen the beginning of an explanation. But Poe's interest in abstract reason is too striking a phenomenon, running as it does not only through his fiction but through his criticism as well and leading him into all sorts of bypaths including cryptography, not to be somehow fundamental in his mental make-up. It is paradoxical and it demands investigation.

Soon after he commenced writing for the *Messenger* his criticism began to show a tendency to depend upon the logical analysis of certain conceptions, and this tendency developed to such an extent that one of his most famous critical writings, *The Philosophy of Composition*, is rather a highly ingenious exercise in the art of rationalization than literary criticism in the ordinary sense;

but before he had discovered this particular field for the exercise of this aspect of his talent he had already given many illustrations of the tendency to absorb himself in problems which demanded for their solution great mental ingenuity without requiring any of that knowledge of life or that understanding of human motives which would be necessary for the treatment of the problems of character in those styles of fiction and criticisms which Poe never wrote.

In the issue of the *Messenger* for April 1836 appeared Poe's essay *Maelzel's Chess-Player*, which furnishes the first extended example of the author's skill in what he called ratiocination and which is marked by the most elaborately methodical exposition. Poe begins by comparing this alleged machine which plays chess with human opponents with certain other famous automata of which accounts have been left, and in a passage worth quoting as an illustration of the perfect clarity of which the author of so much that is fantastic and super-rational was capable, he explains his reason for concluding that it is not an automaton at all:

"But if these machines were ingenious, what shall we think of the calculating machine of Mr. Babbage? What shall we think of an engine of wood and metal which can not only compute astronomical and navigation tables to any given extent, but render the exactitude of its operations mathematically certain through its power of correcting its possible errors? . . . It will, perhaps, be said in reply, that a machine such as we have described is altogether above comparison with the Chess-Player of Maelzel. By no means—it is altogether beneath it—that is to say provided we assume (what should never for a moment be assumed) that the Chess-Player is a *pure machine*, and performs its operations without any immediate human agency. Arithmetical or algebraical calculations are, from their very nature, fixed and determinate. Certain *data* being given, certain results necessarily and inevitably follow. These results have dependence upon nothing, and are influenced by nothing but the *data* originally given. And the question to be solved proceeds or should proceed, to its final determination, by a succession of unerring steps liable to no change, and subject to no modification. This being the case, we can without difficulty conceive the *possibility* of so arranging a piece of mechanism, that upon starting it in accordance with the *data* of the question to be solved, it should continue its movements regularly, progressively, and undeviatingly towards the required solution, since these movements, however complex, are never imagined to be otherwise than finite and determinate. But the case is widely different with the Chess-Player. With him there is no determinate progression. No one move in chess necessarily follows upon any one other. From no particular disposition of the men at one period of the game can we predict their disposition at a different period. Let us place the *first move* in a game of chess, in juxtaposition with the *data* of an algebraic question, and their great difference will be immediately perceived. From the latter—from the *data*—the second step of the question, dependent thereupon, inevitably follows. It is modelled by the *data*. It must be *thus* and not otherwise. But from the first move in the game of chess no especial second move follows of necessity. In the algebraic question, as it proceeds towards solution, the *cer-*

tainty of its operations remains altogether unimpaired. The second step having been a consequence of the *data*, the third step is equally a consequence of the second, the fourth of the third, the fifth of the fourth, and so on, *and not possibly otherwise* to the end. But in proportion to the progress made in a game of chess, is the *uncertainty* of each ensuing move. A few moves having been made, *no* step is certain. Different spectators of the game would advise different moves. All is then dependent upon the variable judgment of the players. Now even granting (what should not be granted) that the movements of the Automaton Chess-Player were in themselves determinate, they would be necessarily interrupted and disarranged by the indeterminate will of his antagonist. There is then no analogy whatever between the operation of the Chess-Player and those of the calculating machine of Mr. Babbage, and if we choose to call the former a *pure machine*, we must be prepared to admit that it is, beyond all comparison, the most wonderful of the inventions of mankind. . . . But it is needless to dwell upon this point. It is quite certain that the operations of the Automaton are regulated by *mind*, and by nothing else."

After this passage, less remarkable for the obvious truth of the facts, which might, indeed, have occurred to any person with a moderately analytical mind, than for the clarity with which the principle is explained, Poe proceeds to an examination of the appearance of the contrivance and the manner in which the exhibition of it is conducted, from which he concludes in what portion the operator is hidden and how he conducts himself. His explanation is thoroughly convincing, and even though he did borrow some facts for the general discussion of automata from Brewster's *Letters on Natural Magic* it is a remarkable achievement by a man whose fancy was as heated as Poe's, and it may well be considered as the first of his detective stories since it is the first of his writings which bases itself not upon dreams nor upon pseudo-science but upon the logical faculty alone.

The piece, which is of considerable length, occupying as it does some thirty pages in Harrison's edition, was obviously written *con amore,* but it was not until exactly five years later that there appeared in the issue of *Graham's Magazine* for April 1841 *The Murders in the Rue Morgue,* a detective story in which Poe managed to combine his characteristic macabre with a very elaborate representation of logical analysis and in which he drew for the first time the character who appears in several stories and who takes his place alongside of the heroes described in the last chapter as the only other male type which Poe invented. A sort of dehumanized thinking-machine, he is represented as a man in whom no interest and no faculties remain except those which are concerned with pure logic, and thus, though he is like the earlier type in that he is completely inhuman, he is the exact opposite in that instead of being one whose fantastic imagination is leading him on through mysticism to insanity he had divested himself of all imagination and all human fallibility and become a sort of logical engine which deals with the *data* furnished by human events in much the same way that Poe imagined Babbage's proposed calculating machine to deal with the *data* of a mathematical problem. Poe's own effort to solve cryp-

tograms and the attitude which he assumed in discussing
them make it evident that he wished to identify himself
with this character exactly in the same manner that he
identified himself with Roderick Usher and his prototypes,
and the fact is of obvious importance in his mental history—but of that more in a more appropriate place.

Doubtless nothing contributed to a greater extent
than did Poe's connection with cryptography to the
growth of the legend which pictured him as a man at
once below and above ordinary human nature; but the
whole subject is still unfortunately wrapped in some obscurity, and it is impossible to be sure of the facts as
distinguished from his own report of them.

Three months after the appearance of *The Murders
in the Rue Morgue* he published in *Graham's Magazine*
for July 1841 an article called *A Few Words on Secret
Writing* which was followed in August, October and December by supplementary articles on the same subject.
In the first of these articles the author discusses various
sorts of secret alphabets ranging from those which con-
sist simply of arbitrary symbols assigned to the various
letters, to other systems constructed upon a much more
intricate plan, and he makes reference to other writings
of his own upon the subject, one of which appeared "in
one of the weekly papers of this city—about eighteen
months ago," and the other in connection with a book-
review in the April number of *Graham's*.

Now the first of these articles was never found by any
of the editors of Poe's works and has never been reprinted; but though no complete file of the periodical
in question is known to exist some numbers are extant
and in one of them is an article on enigmas which does

challenge the reader to submit an example of secret writing in which an arbitrary symbol is substituted for each letter of the alphabet. It is not, however, possible to check up on Poe's later statement that in response to this challenge "Letters were poured in upon the editor from all parts of the country" and were in every case successfully read in spite of the fact that many violated the conditions imposed and one employed seven distinct alphabets in the course of a single communication. Indeed, the fact that *Alexander's Weekly Messenger*, the paper in question, was exceedingly obscure and very short-lived, coupled with the fact that the second and similar challenge in the very prominent *Graham's Magazine* certainly brought much less response, makes legitimate a suspicion that Poe's statement embodies a considerable exaggeration.

This second challenge, also, did certainly appear; and in connection with a secret code said to have been employed by the Duchess of Berry and consisting of the letters of the phrase *Le gouvernement provisoire* substituted in order for the letters of the alphabet, Poe wrote: "Anyone who will take the trouble may address us a note in the same manner as here proposed, and the key phrase may be either in French, Italian, Spanish, German, Latin, or Greek (or in any of the dialects of these languages), and we pledge ourselves for the solution of the riddle." This challenge, says Poe, was accepted by but one person, who sent two cryptograms but declined to give more than the initials of his name; and the solution of these two messages are printed in the July article referred to, along with some discussion of their difficulty. In August he publishes a letter from F. W. Thomas enclosing a cryptogram by a Dr. Frailey, and in the same issue two other letters from Thomas and Frailey acknowledging the correctness of the solution sent to them privately. Poe then publishes the cryptogram itself and offers a year's subscription to anyone who will solve it.

The October number contains the solution of another puzzle sent by a reader, and in the December number Poe printed both a statement to the effect that the prize offer had been won by a Mr. Richard Bolton of Pontotoc, Mississippi, and a communication from another correspondent who outlined a scheme for a yet more intricate cypher. This Poe does not attempt to solve, but adds some more reflections on the general topic and declares that for lack of time he must now consider the whole subject closed.

Thus concluded the whole incident, of which, perhaps, somewhat too much has been made. Poe makes the detailed solution of what he himself had described as the simplest sort of cryptogram the basis of a detective story, *The Gold Bug,* and in the course of a review of *Barnaby Rudge* published in February 1842 he refers to a previous article which (so he says) contained an outline of the plot of the whole novel arrived at by deduction from the opening instalments before the rest had been printed. But, though the *idea* of a thinking machine continued to haunt him and gave rise not only to more detective stories and to that curious article upon literary composition by a logical method, he made no other attempts to realize this ideal in the events of his real life as distinguished from the dream life which gave birth to Dupin the perfect solver of riddles by the employment of infallible reason.

Just how much of this mysterious power was real and how much pretense it is impossible, as we have said, to determine, and it is extremely unfortunate that the results, if any, of the article in *Alexander's Weekly Messenger* cannot be traced. It is unfortunate also that the only explanation of his method which he gives, that contained in *The Gold Bug*, applies only to the simplest sort of cryptogram, and that he nowhere discusses the method employed in solving the more complicated ones. There is no good reason, however, for doubting that the subject did absorb a good deal of his attention and that he had at least a considerable proficiency in dealing with riddles of this class. Moreover, when taken in connection with the fact that his own practice in ingenious deduction was accompanied by the imaginative development in the detective stories of the character of an ideal ratiocinator, it is significant, in connection with his tendency already so firmly insisted upon, to parallel his life and his fiction in such a way as to make his acts and his imagination the two phases of an attempt to realize the same ideal. Dupin like Roderick Usher is the projection of a fancied self, the imaginative realization of a neurotic goal.

No one who has ever sought in cards, in chess, or in cross word puzzles a temporary escape from some pressing anxiety or sorrow will find it hard to understand how Poe, to whom life was perpetual, half understood torture, should have found a mode of escape by occupying himself with ingenuities which have the property of

completely occupying the intellect without either en-
gaging the passions or serving to remind one at any
point of a world full of human dissonances. It is easy
too to see how the reputation so gained would serve to
heighten the color of his legend and make it easier for
him to pose as a man superior to others by virtue of
mysterious powers; but neither of these causes, subsidiary though they undoubtedly are, is quite sufficient
to explain the mania for rationality which developed
in Poe. In the course of the articles on cryptography
his speculations went far beyond the concrete demon-
strations which he affords. "Human ingenuity," he declared triumphantly, "could not devise a cypher which
human ingenuity could not solve"; and when a little later
he turned to write an article professing to explain his
own method of literary composition, so enthusiastic had
he become over the idea of ratiocination that he declared
that imagination in the ordinary sense had nothing to
do with the matter and that he achieved all his most
bizarre effects by a method of coldly rational calculation.

In attempting to understand the meaning of Poe's determined attempt to deny the visionary character of his
work, it is useful to note the steps by which the idea
developed itself. Beginning as a specific attempt to
solve a certain problem in *Maelzel's Chess-Player*, it later
generated the rational detective, and then after this
character was developed in fiction came the identification
of it with the author himself, who attempted to prove
in a literary essay that he was merely Dupin turned
author. Readers might suspect that such grotesque
fantasies as Poe's were the product of a somewhat dis-

ordered mind, but he could prove that they were born
not of fancy but of logic.

Dupin, who is to become, almost equally with Roderick
Usher, Poe's imaginative realization of a neurotic goal,
first appears in *The Murders in the Rue Morgue*, and he
bears in some respects an obvious resemblance to previous heroes. Like so many of the others this young
man comes from a once illustrious family, but "by a
variety of untoward events" he has been reduced to such
poverty that the energy of his character has succumbed
beneath it and he has "ceased to better himself in the
world, or to care for the retrieval of his fortunes." Cut
off from the world by both his misfortunes and his genius,
he can permit himself no luxuries save books, and he is
brought into touch with the teller of the story by the
accident of their both "being in search of the same rare
and very remarkable volume" in an obscure library in
the Rue Montmartre:

"It was at length arranged that we should live together during my stay in the city, and as my worldly
circumstances were somewhat less embarrassed than his
own, I was permitted to be at the expense of renting, and
furnishing in a style which suited the rather fantastic
gloom of our common temper, a time-eaten and grotesque
mansion, long deserted through superstitions into which
we did not enquire, and tottering to its fall in a retired
and desolate portion of the Faubourg St. Germain.

"Had the routine of our life at this place been known
to the world, we should have been regarded as madmen—
although, perhaps, as madmen of a harmless nature.
Our seclusion was perfect. We admitted no visitors.
Indeed the locality of our retirement had been carefully

kept secret from my own former associates; and it had been many years since Dupin had ceased to know or be known in Paris. We existed in ourselves alone.

"It was a freak of fancy in my friend (for what else shall I call it?) to be enamored of Night for her own sake; and into this *bizarrerie* as into all his others, I quietly fell; giving myself up to his wild whims with a perfect *abandon*. The sable divinity would not herself dwell with us always; but we could counterfeit her presence. At the first dawn of the morning we closed all the many shutters of our old building: lighted a couple of tapers which, strongly perfumed, threw out only the ghastliest and feeblest of rays. By the aid of these we then busied ourselves in dreams—reading, writing, or conversing, until warned by the clock of the advent of the true darkness. Then we sallied forth into the streets, arm and arm, continuing the topics of the day, or roaming far and wide until a late hour, seeking, amid the wild lights and shadows of the populous city, the infinity of mental excitement which quiet observation can afford."

It is not difficult to recognize in all this the essential traits of the picture which the imagination of Poe continually drew and which was described in the preceding chapter. Whenever he set his imagination to work to conceive a way of life his imagination almost invariably produced spontaneously and from its own desires the fantasy which is here represented, even down to the strongly perfumed tapers whose ghastly and feeble rays illuminate with appropriately fitful light the grotesque *décor*. As the present story proceeds, however, it suddenly differentiates itself sharply from the other type.

Hitherto the speculations of the stock hero, delirious and usually but vaguely specified, are associated generally with a disease of mind and body. They deal with mystic conceptions and they frequently prepare the way for supernatural events, but now Poe, as though he had grown himself frightened by his habitual tendency to slide into something perilously like madness, invents an ideal of super-rationality which gives to his hero an air quite as inhuman as before but removes from him at the same time any suspicion of delirium.

Upon one of his nocturnal walks, Dupin suddenly turns to his companion with the remark: "He is a very little fellow, that's true, and would do better for the *Théâtre des Variétés*," and so takes the latter off his guard that he replies before he realizes that, not having uttered any of the thoughts to which this comment applies, his thoughts have, apparently, been read by the mysterious Dupin. The latter, however, immediately assures him that the apparent marvel has a rational explanation. The actor in question, Chantilly by name, is, it seems, an ex-cobbler, and some fifteen minutes before Dupin's companion had collided in the street with a fruiterer. Dupin has traced the train of association in his friend's mind in the following manner:

"As we crossed into this street, a fruiterer with a large basket upon his head, brushing quickly past us, thrust you upon a pile of paving-stones collected at a spot where the causeway is undergoing repair. You stepped upon one of the loose fragments, slipped, slightly strained your ankle, appeared vexed or sulky, muttered a few words, turned to look at the pile, and then proceeded in silence. I was not particularly attentive to what you did; but observation has become with me, of late, a species of necessity.

"You kept your eyes upon the ground—glancing, with a petulant expression, at the holes and ruts in the pavement, (so that I saw you were still thinking of the stones,) until we reached the little alley called Lamartine, which has been paved, by way of experiment, with the overlapping and riveted blocks. Here your countenance brightened up, and perceiving your lips move, I could not doubt that you murmured the word 'stereotomy,' a term very affectedly applied to this species of pavement. I knew that you could not say to yourself 'stereotomy' without being brought to think of atomies, and thus of the theories of Epicurus; and since, when we discussed this subject not very long ago, I mentioned to you how singularly, yet with how little notice, the vague guesses of that noble Greek had met with confirmation in the late nebular cosmogony, I felt that you could not avoid casting your eyes upward to the great *nebula* in Orion, and I certainly expected that you would do so. You did look up; and I was now assured that I had correctly followed your steps. But in that bitter *tirade* upon Chantilly, which appeared in yesterday's '*Musée*,' the satirist, making some disgraceful allusions to the cobbler's change of name upon assuming the buskin, quoted a line about which we have often conversed. I mean the line

Perdidit antiquum litera prima sonum.

I had told you that this was in reference to Orion, formerly written Urion; and, from certain pungencies connected with this explanation, I was aware that you could

111

not have forgotten it. It was clear, therefore, that you would not fail to combine the two ideas of Orion and Chantilly. That you did combine them I saw by the character of the smile which passed over your lips. You thought of the poor cobbler's immolation. So far, you had been stooping in your gait; but now I saw you draw yourself up to your full height; I was then sure that you reflected upon the diminutive figure of Chantilly. At this point I interrupted your meditations to remark that as, in fact, he *was* a very little fellow—that Chantilly— he would do better at the *Théâtre des Variétés*."

Now doubtless this passage is sufficiently convincing for highly romantic fiction. One understands so perfectly what it is that the author is saying that one tends in a measure to accept it without question although it requires but an instant's thought to show that its logic is quite as speciously fantastic as any of Poe's confessedly fantastic imaginings. The associations of random thought require so slight and often so unessential connections between succeeding ideas that the possibilities are almost infinite and quite unpredictable. One might, it is true, follow the line indicated in the present case but there is no point at which the stream might not have diverged in any one of a hundred different directions since though Dupin knew a portion of the content of his friend's memory he was totally unaware of innumerable other associations which were equally probable. Here Poe's imagination had been fired by the idea of power which is associated with the possession of the logical faculties exactly as it had been formerly fired by the idea of power associated with scientific knowledge, and without caring any more for real logic than he cared for real science he has imaginatively identified himself with a character endowed with this power to a superhuman degree. He did it is true make some actual experiments in cryptography, though just how extensive these were is still a matter of doubt, but he soon abandoned them because he was able through the force of his imagination to obtain from fancy, less laboriously and more completely, all the satisfaction which the actual practice of the powers of deduction could give. He continued to discuss in the abstract and with great ingenuity various abstruse subjects. He would prove that checkers called into play higher mental faculties than chess or he would enlarge upon the limitations of mathematical reasoning, but he was certainly no mathematician and, so far as I know, he never gave any unusual amount of time to any game. Inventing problems which his super-detective could solve and inventing elaborate ex-post-facto explanations of the process by which his own works were written, he played at being a logical genius in exactly the same way that he played at being a scientist.

It is pretty generally agreed that the attempt which Poe made in *The Philosophy of Composition* to convey the impression that all his own works were the result of logical and deliberate contrivance is either a conscious or an unconscious hoax. There are *a priori* objections to the belief that in general artistic works are created thus, but there is no writer who ever lived who seems less likely than Poe to have created in this way. In the management of his own life he was, as we have already seen and shall see again, moved almost always by prejudice, passion, or perversity and almost never by reason. His works, characterized at their best by the fantastic il-

113

logicality of dreams, are such as no man could contrive, and so uniformly similar in content and effect as to prove that they must in a sense have written themselves since no one who was struggling for bread and knew that a monotony of horror was complained of against him would willingly repeat himself so often when he could, according to his own statement, proceed to produce in story or poem whatever effect he chose to select. When it is remembered also that the characters in his stories and poems are frequently suffering from disorders of the mind of exactly the sort which might give rise to fancies such as those amidst which they are represented, that Poe's works are replete with various *obiter dicta* upon the subject of obsessions, perversions, and manias which he could have learned of only from himself, and that he gave in the mysterious wreck of his own life proof of the intimate relationship to the characters which he created, it is impossible not to see that instead of being deliberately invented his stories and poems invented themselves.

"I say to myself, in the first place, 'Of the innumerable effects, or impressions, of which the heart, the intellect, or (more generally) the soul is susceptible, what one shall I, on the present occasion, select?' " So Poe writes. But the fact remains that though he may have succeeded in convincing himself that he made such a choice, something unconscious within him saw to it he should "choose" always an effect which belonged to a very small class of the "innumerable" effects of which he speaks and which was moreover one which is rarely felt by any except persons of markedly abnormal mind. He chose perhaps but his choice was never more than between the indulgence of this or of that neurotic fantasy, between the embodiment of this or of that idealization of his own traits and capacities.

There is, however, good reason for believing that Poe, whose genius consisted, perhaps, in the possession to an extraordinary degree of the faculty of rationalization, which is one of the distinguishing characteristics of all neurotics, succeeded in convincing himself, at times at least, that he was the mere logical engine which he liked to imagine, and one may find both the roots of this delusion and the origin of the need which generated it at a time before Dupin had been created or *The Philosophy of Composition* written. The preface to the volume of collected stories called *Tales of the Grotesque and Arabesque* contains the following passage of significant self-defense:

"The epithets 'Grotesque' and 'Arabesque' will be found to indicate with sufficient precision the prevalent tenor of the tales here published. But from the fact that, during a period of some two or three years, I have written five-and-twenty short stories whose general character may be so briefly defined, it cannot be fairly inferred—at all events it is not truly inferred—that I have, for this species of writing, any inordinate, or indeed any particular taste or prepossession. I may have written with an eye to republication in volume form, and may, therefore, have desired to preserve, as far as a certain point, a certain unity of design. That is, indeed, the fact; and it may even happen that, in this manner, I shall never compose anything again. I speak of these things here, because I am led to think that it is this prevalence of the 'Arabesque' in my serious tales,

115

which has induced one or two critics to tax me, in all friendliness, with what they have pleased to term 'Germanism' and gloom. The charge is in bad taste, and the grounds of it have not been sufficiently considered. Let us admit, for the moment, that the 'phantasy-pieces' now given *are* Germanic, or what not. Then Germanism is 'in the vein' for the time being. To-morrow I may be anything but German, as yesterday I was everything else. These many pieces are yet one book. My friends would be quite as wise in taxing an astronomer with too much astronomy, or an ethical writer with treating too largely of morals. But the truth is that, with a single exception, there is no one of these stories in which the scholar would recognize the distinctive features of that species of pseudo-horror which we are taught to call Germanic, for no better reason than that some of the secondary names of German literature have become identified with its folly. If in many of my productions terror has been the thesis, I maintain that terror is not of Germany, but of the soul—that I have deduced this terror only from its legitimate sources, and urged it only to its legitimate results."

It is evident from this passage that Poe resented the implication that his imagination could generate nothing except horror, and it is probable that this resentment was not unmixed with fear. Notwithstanding the suggestion that he might perhaps never write again in the same manner, he was constrained in spite of himself to do so and thus to be brought closer and closer to a realization of his perilous position upon the brink of madness. There must have been times when he knew that the "effects" which he liked to imagine himself as de-

liberately choosing were in fact thrust upon him, moments when he realized that in giving such vividly
intimate pictures of temporary insanity in *Berenice*, of
sadism in *The Black Cat*, or of mad obsession in *The
Tell-Tale Heart* he was confessing to himself and others
the giddy instability of his own mind. Mrs. Whitman
remembered a penciled note appended to a manuscript
copy of one of Poe's later poems which read "All that
I have here expressed was actually present to me. Remember the mental condition which gave rise to 'Ligeia'
—I regard these visions even as they arise, with an awe
which in some measure moderates or tranquilizes the
ecstasy"; and while this confession gives the lie direct to
his published statement concerning his mechanical
method of composition it helps to explain why he himself
should want to believe it.

Just as his whole life was a struggle, conducted with
all the cunning of the unconsciousness, against a realization of the psychic impotence of his sexual nature,
so was it a struggle also against a realization of the mental instability to which the first gave rise. It was a
battle doomed to be lost from the beginning, and shortly
before the final simultaneous dissolution of his mind and
body Poe confessed to at least one fully developed delusion of persecution which will be discussed in its appropriate place; but doubtless he considerably postponed
the final breakdown by means of the ingenious rationalization which convinced him, partly at least, that his imagination was under perfect control.

We must imagine, I think, that Poe, like many others,
first turned to the practice of logic and ingenuity as
an escape from feeling but that he soon found it a

valuable contribution to his legend. To seem a man endowed to a super-human extent with the gift of rationality gratified that thirst for fame of an unusual sort
which we have already noted, and it served at the same
time an additional internal function. As the realization
that he was as a matter of fact the victim of irrational
and uncontrollable emotions gradually forced itself upon
him, he countered this realization with the pretense that
he was, on the contrary, abnormally clear in his mental
processes. He demonstrated the fact as best he could
to both himself and the public by his article upon the
chess-player and his experiments in cryptography, and
then, warming to the subject, he created the character
of Dupin with whom he might imaginatively identify
himself. Finally, he attempted in *The Philosophy of
Composition* to convince himself that all his previous
work had been the result of this same rational faculty
to which he now clung desperately as the proof of his
sanity, and thus the process was complete. First reasoning in order to escape feeling and then seizing upon the
idea of reason as an explanation of the mystery of his
own character, Poe invented the detective story in order
that he might not go mad.

VI

THE BRANDY NOSED MR. BRIGGS

THE difficulty of writing a biographical study of Poe consists in the difficulty of establishing a relationship between the events of his life and his writings. Though the tales and the poetry which he wrote are in their way so intensely personal, the line is sharply drawn between these confessions made under the disguise of fiction and the things which he wrote or said frankly in *propria persona*. The bulk of his earlier letters are frankly silent upon all except external affairs, and he never, it is clear, unburdened his soul to anyone (not even to the two devoted but intellectually undistinguished women who supported his life) until he was approaching the end of his career and no longer his real self. To tell the story of his wretched life and to punctuate it with the notices of his published work is to produce two records between which no essential connection is clear and which throw but little light upon one another. He wandered from city to city, living now in this and now in that humble quarter and holding for a short time editorial positions which he could never keep upon this or that magazine, but his work showed but little change as he moved from place to place.

Having come to Richmond in the Summer of 1835 and having assumed shortly after the editorship of the *Messenger*, his associations with it was ended before January 1837 for some reason unknown but doubtless connected with fits of intemperance to which letters addressed to him by his friends give evidence. He moved to New York where he inhabited for a short time a wooden shanty on Carmine Street and where the indefatigable Mrs. Clemm again took boarders. In 1838 he went with his family to Philadelphia where two editorial engagements—ending in the inevitable disagreement—helped to maintain him until he returned to New York in 1844 and began the final phase of his life. Yet save for the literary portraits which he published during this final phase neither persons nor places seem to have influenced or even touched him, and there is no reason to suppose that his work would have been essentially different had he spent all of his years as editor of the Richmond magazine. Wherever he went he carried his universe with him, since only the half understood anguish of his soul and the fancies which it generated were real to him. Locked tight within this universe, he was barely aware of physical movement and beyond the reach of possible influence from persons or places. "The realities of the world affected me as visions, and as visions only, while the wild ideas of the land of dreams became, in turn,—not the material of my every-day existence—but in very deed that existence utterly and solely in itself." Even the death of his wife, to whom he was attached with all the intensity of a morbid passion, can hardly, though it doubtless hastened his death, be said to have influenced his work in any particular way, since she was always dead in his imagination and figured usually as dead in those tales or poems which are woven around her or, rather, round the phantom which she represented. "The lost Lenore" over whom so many dirges were said was yet still alive in reality when they were written, though she had been always dead in those visions which become "not the material of every-day existence—but in very deed that existence utterly and solely in itself."

To Mrs. Clemm alone belongs the credit of keeping him physically alive. A woman born to devote herself unthinkingly to the humble service of others, she attached herself to her simple-minded daughter and incalculable foster son with all the unquestioning devotion of a mother to a wayward child. Wherever they went and through whatever difficulties they passed she kept up a relentless and perfectly matter-of-fact struggle to keep starvation from the door. She tended her boarders when boarders were to be had, she went from editor to editor with the manuscripts which she could not understand, and she was even seen, in the desperate last years, plucking dandelions in the fields around Fordham in order that she might thus supplement the scant food upon her table; and if she was ever either out of patience with Edgar in his fits of intemperance or frightened by the terrible depths of his melancholy she never confessed the fact to any soul. Calmly assuming his genius, she never questioned either the greatness of his talents or the goodness of his character for the reason that to her, as to many women like her, neither was a matter of great importance. She was attached to him as a human being to be loved, and she had no need of judging.

Poe accepted her devotion in exactly the spirit in which it was offered. When he was away from her he wrote concerning every detail of his outward life—explaining for example that since it was raining he had bought an umbrella for twenty-five cents—and when he was with her he depended utterly upon her ministrations, receiving from her hand a cup of coffee every half hour while he was writing, or walking with her for hours in the starlight while she, hiding the shivers which the cold night air brought on, listened to his explanation of the cosmos. To Didier she said: "Eddie had no idea of the value of money. I had to attend to all of his pecuniary affairs. I even bought his clothes for him; he never bought a pair of gloves or a cravat for himself." Yet she never spoke of him except in terms of the greatest affection. "He loved Virginia with a tenderness and devotion which no words can express, and he was the most affectionate of sons to me," she said. When toward the end he returned to her after a fit of drunken madness she wrote only: "God has heard my prayers and once more returned my poor, darling Eddy to me. But how *changed!* I scarcely knew him. I was nearly distracted at not hearing from him. I knew *something* dreadful had occurred. And oh! how near I was to losing him! But our good and gracious God *saved* him. The blood about my heart becomes cold when I think of it."

Any estimate of Poe's character, for the making of which there is, as we shall see, a sufficiency of damning evidence in the story of his relationships with the outside world, would be completely one-sided if it failed to take into account the testimony of this woman to whom he seems to have revealed all that was best in him. Completely inconsistent as to character, he could be quarrelsome, unreasonable, and rancorous in his dealings with those whom he met outside the charmed circle of the home where he was completely sheltered from reality; but within that little realm where he and his will

MARIA CLEMM

From a daguerreotype taken in 1849

were supreme and where he was never brought into contact with the things he refused to admit, the sweetness which seems to have been his normal character but which was completely perverted by his mental disease was alone evident. None of the people who saw him there draw any save an idyllic picture of the poverty- and disease-stricken household held together by mutual love, and even after making all due allowance for the forbearance of Mrs. Clemm there can be no doubt that she knew a man essentially different from the one whose hatred of the world, almost demoniacal in its intensity, constantly recoiled upon himself.

Yet it was in his pathetic little home, where he was at his gentlest and best, that he dreamed his most terrible dreams. While Mrs. Clemm bustled about the every-day affairs of the household and while Virginia babbled pleasantly with the childishness of arrested development or lay gasping in one of her periodic illnesses, the shades of a grandiose madness settled around him, and of this life we have a double record—the record of its external events as they were observed by people who saw him live it and the record of its intensest inward moments as set down by Poe himself.

Outwardly all was more peaceful than a household so overcome by poverty might be expected to be. "For eight months or more 'one house contained us as one table fed,' " wrote a man who boarded with Mrs. Clemm during the New York period. "During that time I saw much of him, and had an opportunity of conversing with him often, and I must say, that I never saw him the least affected with liquor nor ever descend to any known vice while he was one of the most courteous, gentlemanly and intelligent companions I have met with during my journeyings and haltings through diverse divisions of the globe." And he was, so Mrs. Clemm herself testifies, "domestic in all his habits, seldom leaving home for an hour unless his darling Virginia, or myself were with him. He was truly an affectionate, kind husband, and a devoted son to me. He was impulsive, generous, affectionate and *noble*. His tastes were very simple, and his admiration for all that was good and beautiful very great.—We three lived only for each other." And to this fact even Griswold bears witness when he writes:

"It was while he resided in Philadelphia that I became acquainted with him.

"His manner, except during his fits of intoxication, was very quiet and gentlemanly. He was usually dressed with simplicity and elegance, and when once he sent for me to visit him, during a period of illness caused by protracting and anxious watching at the side of his sick wife, I was impressed by the singular neatness and the air of refinement in his home."

Yet in the midst of this idyllically peaceful household Poe lived in a world of gloomy magnificence and unspeakable horror. His wife, clung to because he lived by the illusion which she supplied, was the one island of peace, and in rare moments like that which produced *Eleonora* she could be the center of a brief dream of beauty in which he inhabited with her the Valley of the Many-Colored Grass. "No unguided footsteps ever came upon the vale; for it lay far away up among a range of giant hills that hung beetling about it, shutting out the sunlight from its sweetest recesses. . . . Thus it was that we lived all alone, knowing nothing of the world

without the valley,—I, and my cousin and her mother."
But such sweet dreams were rare, and even Virginia was
assimilated generally into the gloomy fate-stricken figures
of Berenice, Morella, Ligeia or the Lady Madeline, and
the idyll became a tragedy precipitated by madness or
disease.

Yet when this saving figure was not present the dreams
grew more gross and more horrible. The images which
presented themselves were invariably of madness and
crime. A malignant dwarf burns alive the courtiers who
represent the world which has wronged him, in a dungeon
of the Inquisition a prisoner suffers a crescendo of tortures, a man is walled living into a tomb, a fiend gouges
out the eyes of a cat, and a murderer pounces upon an
old man in the night to kill him because of his glittering
eye. As the incidents, so too are the thoughts which accompany them. In his cozy retreat, protected from the
annoyances of every-day life and cheered by the wife
whom he adores, Poe meditates upon terrible things.
There was, so far as one could judge, no touch of kindred
morbidity in either Mrs. Clemm or her daughter. Poe
needed no suggestion from the outside world, for, living
in his own universe, none of his actual experiences are
real enough to appear anywhere in the works of his imagination but perversities in horrible variety crowd upon
him. He writes, as a preliminary to a story, an essay
upon the fascination which the idea of premature burial
has for him; he speculates upon that spirit of the perverse which leads one to do a thing for no other reason
except that it is wrong, and doubtless he knows in his
own person those horrible lapses of consciousness which
he describes so vividly in *Berenice*. Now he fancies him-

self as one of those men who "die nightly in their beds,
wringing the hands of ghostly confessors, and looking
them piteously in the eyes—die with despair of heart
and convulsion of throat, on account of the hideousness
of mysteries which will not *suffer themselves* to be revealed" because their consciousness has taken up "a
burthen of horror so heavy that it can be thrown down
only into the grave," and in his imagination he wanders like The Man of the Crowd whom "it will be in vain
to follow; for I shall learn no more of him, nor of his
deeds. The worst heart of the world is a grosser book
than the 'Hortulus Animæ' and perhaps it is but one
of the great mercies of God that *es lässt sich nicht lesen.*"
Now he feels himself gripped by the irrational hate of
the hero of *The Tell-Tale Heart,* and "it is impossible,"
he explains, "to say how first the idea entered by brain;
but once conceived, it haunted me day and night. Object
there was none. Passion there was none. I loved the
old man. He had never wronged me. He had never
given me insult. For his gold I had no desire. I think
it was his eye! yes, it was this! He had the eye of a
vulture—a pale blue eye, with a film over it. Whenever it fell upon me, my blood ran cold; and so by degrees—very gradually—I made up my mind to take the
life of the old man, and thus rid myself of the eye forever." And again, as in *The Black Cat* or that terrible
story so often before referred to in which the lover in
a fit of unconsciousness mutilates his mistress in order
to rob her of her teeth, he understands from the promptings of his own soul that dangerous alchemy, not investigated by scientists until Poe had lain many years in

126

his grave, by which love is transformed into **bloody** hate:

"To muse for long unwearied hours, with my attention riveted to some frivolous device on the margin, or in the typography of a book; to become absorbed for the better part of a summer's day, in a quaint shadow falling aslant upon the tapestry, or upon the floor; to lose myself for an entire night in watching the steady flame of a lamp, or the embers of a fire; to dream away whole days over the perfume of a flower; to repeat monotonously, some common word, until the sound, by dint of frequent repetition, ceased to convey any idea whatever to the mind; to lose all sense of motion or of physical existence, by means of absolute bodily quiescence long and obstinately persevered in;—such," he confesses in *Berenice*, "were a few of the most common and least pernicious vagaries induced by a condition of the mental faculties, not, indeed, altogether unparalleled, but certainly bidding defiance to anything like analysis or explanation." And in the midst of such lonely horrors he had nothing with which to comfort him except the hope that madness and the highest wisdom were one:

"I am come of a race noted for vigor of fancy and ardor of passion. Men have called me mad; but the question is not yet settled, whether madness is or is not the loftiest intelligence—whether much that is glorious—whether all that is profound—does not spring from disease of thought—from *moods* of minds exalted at the expense of general intellect. They who dream by day are cognizant of many things which escape those who dream only by night. In their gray visions they obtain glimpses of eternity, and thrill, in awaking, to find that they have been upon the verge of the great secret. In snatches, they learn something of the wisdom which is of good, and more of the mere knowledge which is of evil. They penetrate, however rudderless or compassless, into the vast ocean of the 'light ineffable; and again, like the adventures of the Nubian geographer, *'agressi sunt mare tenebrarum, quid en eo esset exploraturi.'*

"We will say, then, that I am mad."

Doubtless it was because he was so completely the center of this domestic universe that Poe exhibited in it so few of the outward signs of his complete maladjustment to the world of reality. Here his will was law; no one ever questioned his supremacy or doubted his transcendent genius, and the world seemed to revolve around him. His home furnished an escape as complete as his imagination and he could retire into it as he retired into one of his visions for he could find in either the two things necessary to his peace—the sexless phantom and the illusion of unquestionable supremacy. When, however, he was obliged to make any contact with the outside world there arose the inevitable conflict between beneficent illusion and wounding actuality. Editors, for example, would not play the game which Virginia and Mrs. Clemm were willing to play. Suddenly some word or action would remind him that he was not all his fancy pictured him, that mankind at large was not aware of the shadowy domain where he was master of castles of gloomy magnificence and possessed of strange inhuman knowledge lifting him above the mortal level. From this realization would come anguish, and something like madness would arise from the conflict between what were to him two equally vivid realities. From this madness would spring the burning irrational anger, the seemingly petty malice of the occasional deed of deliberate dishonesty which amazed those who knew his better self and which convinced the casual acquaintance that his nature was essentially evil.

Once his anger was aroused he forgot all the gentleness which others praised in him and all the gentlemanliness of which he was so proud. When his pride was touched, when he felt himself personally wronged, his anger knew no bounds and expressed itself with a childishly unrestrained fury. Thus he referred in an open letter published in a Philadelphia newspaper to "the brandy-nose of Mr. Briggs (since Mr. Briggs is only one-third described when his nose is omitted) and to the family resemblance between the whole visage of Mr. English and that of the best-looking but most unprincipled of Mr. Barnum's baboons." And in another letter concerning William E. Burton who, as owner of *The Gentleman's Magazine* had certainly befriended Poe but with whom there had been some quarrel as the result, apparently, of Poe's intemperance, he writes: "In regard to Burton . . . the situation is embarrassing. It is impossible, as you say, to notice a buffoon and a felon, as one gentleman would notice another." Poe was wronged as every genius who does not find a ready market for itself is wronged; more than that, he was certainly defamed by those with whom he quarreled but there is no denying either that he made a ready second in any quarrel or that there were traits of his character which made it easy for the world to misjudge him.

Nothing will illustrate better the apparently unpardonable rudeness of which he could be capable or serve better to explain the curious mental twists which justified it to himself than the affair of his public reading in Boston. In 1845 when he had reached nearly the height of his fame he was invited with every gesture of courtesy to read a poem before the Boston Lyceum. The invitation which came, apparently, through the suggestion of Lowell might very well be interpreted as a motion on the part of the inhabitants of the recognized center of American letters to receive Poe into the group from which his exclusion had been the cause of much bitterness on his part, and if he felt, as he might well have done, that he preferred not to join the ranks of the traditionally acceptable writers he could at least have refused with the same politeness with which he was asked. Instead, however, of doing anything of the sort he accepted; and when he appeared upon the platform he read, not the new poem which was expected of him, but, and without any explanation, an excerpt from his early and nearly incomprehensible work *Al Aaraaf* which had been published in the volume of 1829. The result was that his auditors left the hall in bewilderment or anger, that the Boston newspapers denounced him, and that he retorted from New York in the most violently insulting manner.

Now if these facts stood alone, Poe's action might be set down as the result simply of incredibly bad judgment but he took good care to let it be known that he wished his action to be regarded as a calculated insult and thus he published abroad the fact that after he had accepted a polite invitation extended in good faith he,

whose great pride was to be regarded as a Virginia gentleman, was guilty of a premeditated insult. Actually it
is not certain how he came in the first instance to do so
mad a thing. It is said that he found himself unable
to compose the poem which he had expected to deliver,
that he wrote in despair to Mrs. Frances S. Osgood be-
seeching her to compose the poem for him and that,
when she failed to complete her composition, he seized
upon *Al Aaraaf* in a fit of desperation. It is, on the
other hand, stated by Thomas Dunn English that he one
day met Poe just recovering from a spree and that Poe
confessed to him his inability to fulfill the promise he
had made of composing a poem for the occasion.
"Well," said English, according to his account, "write
them that you have been indisposed, because you have
been. I consider it a case of disease in you, and post-
pone the event." "But," replied Poe, "I want the
money." "Well," said English, "you can't get the money
without you earn it." "I'll fix that," replied Poe, and
departed.

A portion of Mrs. Osgood's poem exists and the version of the story which involves her is probably cor-
rect, but there can be no question that after the event
Poe confessed and gloried in deliberate and unpardonable rudeness. A week after his appearance he printed
in the *Broadway Journal* a reply to a paragraph
founded upon a statement in the *Boston Transcript* and
published in a New York paper. From it I shall copy
a rather long extract because it illustrates the childish
aspect of Poe's temper and suggests the obsession which
lay behind this particular exhibition of it.

"Our excellent friend Major Noah has suffered himself to be cajoled by that most beguiling of all beguiling little divinities, Miss Walters, of 'The Transcript.' We have been looking all over her article, with the aid of a taper, to see if we could discover a single syllable of truth in it—and really blush to acknowledge that we cannot. The adorable creature has been telling a parcel of fibs about us, by way of revenge for something that we did to Mr. Longfellow (who admires her very much) and for calling her 'a pretty little witch' into the bargain.

"The facts of the case seem to be these:—We were invited to 'deliver' (stand and deliver) a poem before the Boston Lyceum. As a matter of course, we accepted the invitation. The audience *was* 'large and distinguished.' Mr. Cushing preceded us with a very capital discourse. He was much applauded. On arising, we were most cordially received. We occupied some fifteen minutes with an apology for not 'delivering,' as is usual in such cases, a didactic poem: A didactic poem, in our opinion, being precisely no poem at all. After some farther words—still of apology—for the 'indefiniteness' and 'general imbecility' of what we had to offer—all so unworthy of a *Bostonian* audience—we commenced, and, with many interruptions of applause, concluded. Upon the whole the approbation was considerably more (the more the pity too) than that bestowed upon Mr. Cushing.

"When we had made an end, the audience, of course, rose to depart—and about one tenth of them, probably, had really departed, when Mr. Coffin, one of the managing committee, arrested those who remained by the announcement that we had been requested to deliver 'The

Raven.' We delivered 'The Raven' forthwith—(without taking a receipt)—were very cordially applauded again —and this was the end of it—with the exception of the sad tale invented to suit her own purposes, by that amiable little enemy of ours, Miss Walters. We shall never call a woman 'a pretty little witch' again, as long as we live.

"We like Boston. We were born there—and perhaps it is just as well not to mention that we are heartily ashamed of the fact. The Bostonians are very well in their way. Their hotels are bad. Their pumpkin pies are delicious. Their poetry is not so good. Their common is no common thing—and the duck pond might answer—if its answer could be heard for the frogs.

"But with all these good qualities the Bostonians have no soul. They have always evinced toward us individually, the basest ingratitude for the services we rendered them in enlightening them about the originality of Mr. Longfellow. When we accepted, therefore, an invitation to 'deliver' a poem in Boston—we accepted it simply and solely, because we had a curiosity to know how it felt to be publicly hissed—and because we wished to see what effect we could produce by a neat little *impromptu* speech in reply. Perhaps, however, we overrated our own importance, or the Bostonian want of common civility—which is not quite so manifest as one or two of their editors would wish the public to believe. We assure Major Noah that he is wrong. The Bostonians are well-bred—as *very* dull persons very generally are.

"Still, with their vile ingratitude staring us in the eyes, it could scarcely be supposed that we would put ourselves

to the trouble of composing for the Bostonians anything in the shape of an *original* poem. We did not.
We had a poem (of about 500 lines) lying before us—
one quite as good as new—one, at all events, that we
considered would answer sufficiently well for an audience
of Transcendentalists. *That* we gave them.—It was
the best we had—for the price—and it *did* answer remarkably well. Its name was *not* 'The Messenger Star'
—who but Miss Walters would ever think of so delicious
a little bit of invention as that? We had *no* name for
it at all. The poem is what is occasionally called a
'juvenile poem'—but the fact is, it is anything but juvenile now, for we wrote it, printed it, and published it,
in book form, before we had fairly completed our tenth
year. [This of course is not true.] We read it *verbatim*, from a copy now in our possession, and which
we shall be happy to show at any moment to any of our
inquisitive friends.

"We do not, ourselves, think the poem a remarkably
good one—it is not sufficiently transcendental. Still it
did well enough for the Boston audience—who evinced
characteristic discrimination in understanding, and especially applauding, all those knotty passages which we
ourselves have not yet been able to understand.

"As regards the anger of the 'Boston Times' and
one or two other absurdities—as regards, we say, the
wrath of Achilles—we incurred it—or rather its manifestation—by letting some of our cat out of the bag a
few hours sooner than we had intended. Over a bottle
of champagne, that night, we confessed to Messrs. Cushing, Whipple, Hudson, Field, and a few other natives
who swear not altogether by the frog-pond—we con-

fessed, we say, the soft impeachment of the hoax. *Et hinc illae irae.* We should have waited a couple of days."

Three weeks later he returned to the subject in another childish outburst:

"Were the question demanded of us—'What is the most exquisite of sublunary pleasures?' we should reply, without hesitation, the making of a fuss, or, in the classical words of a western friend, the 'kicking up a bobbery.' Never was a 'bobbery' more delightful than that which we have just succeeded in 'kicking up' all around about the Boston Common. We never saw the Frog-Pondians so lively in our lives. They seem absolutely upon the point of waking up. In about nine days the puppies may get open their eyes.

"That is to say they may get open their eyes to certain facts which have long been obvious to all the world except themselves—the facts that there exist other cities than Boston—other men of letters than Professor Longfellow—other vehicles of literary information that the 'Down East Review.' . . .

"We had *tact* enough not to be 'taken in and done for' by the Bostonians. *Timeo Danaos et dona ferentes*—(for *timeo* substitute *contemno* or *turn-up-our-nose-o*). We know very well that, among a certain *clique* of Frogpondians, there existed a predetermination to abuse us under *any* circumstances. We knew that, write what we would, they would swear it to be worthless. We knew that were we to compose for them a 'Paradise Lost,' they would pronounce it an indifferent poem. It would have been very weak in us, then, to put ourselves to the trouble of attempting to please these people. We preferred pleasing ourselves. We read before them a 'juvenile'—a *very* 'juvenile' poem—and thus the Frogpondians were *had*—were delivered up to the enemy bound hand and foot. Never were a set of people more completely demolished. They have blustered and flustered—but what have they done or said that has not made them more completely ridiculous?—what, in the name of Momus, is it *possible* for them to do or say?

"We 'delivered,' them the 'juvenile poem' and they received it with applause. This is accounted for by the fact that the *clique* (contemptible in numbers as in everything else) were overruled by the rest of the assembly. These malignants did not dare to interrupt by their preconcerted hisses, the respectful and profound attention of the majority. We have been told, indeed, that as many as three or four of the personal friends of the little old lady entitled Miss Walters, did actually leave the hall during the recitation—but, upon the whole, this was the very best thing they could do. We have been told this, we say,—we did not *see* them take their departure:—the fact is they belong to a class of people that we make it a point *never to see.*

"The poem being thus well received, in spite of this ridiculous little cabal—the next thing to be done was to abuse it in the papers. Here, they imagined, they were sure of their game. But what have they accomplished? The poem, they say is bad. We admit it. We insisted upon the fact in our prefatory remarks, and we insist upon it now, over and over again. It *is* bad—it is wretched—and what then? We wrote it at ten years of age—had it been worth even a pumpkin pie undoubtedly we should not have 'delivered' it to *them*.

"To demonstrate its utter worthlessness 'The Boston Star' . . . has copied the poem in full, with two or three columns of criticism (we suppose) by way of explaining that we should have been hanged for its perpetration. There is no doubt of it whatever—we should. 'The Star,' however, (a dull luminary) has done us more honor that it intended; it has copied our *third* edition of the poem, revised and improved. We considered this too good for the occasion by one-half, and so 'delivered' the *first* edition with all its imperfections on its head. It is the first—the original edition—the *delivered* edition—which we now publish in our collection of Poems."

The world is hardly to be blamed if it judges from such an outburst that Poe, whatever his genius, was hardly to be trusted in polite society. Even the sympathetic student will find it hard to connect the reckless perpetrator of such childish and ill-mannered hoaxes with the sad and gentle figure whose sweetness of character was praised by many who saw him in his calmer moments and it is, indeed, impossible to make the connection except by assuming in him a psychology not wholly rational nor normal. Granted that he was, as unquestionable testimony proves, essentially a gentleman, then some obsession must have seemed to him to justify what to those who know nothing of the obsession is unjustifiable and it is evident that this obsession was a hatred of Boston and Bostonians so intense and profound as to destroy absolutely his sense of justice and decorum.

Poe, as he confesses in the article just quoted, had

been born in Boston and he carried with him all his life a miniature portrait presented him by his mother which bore upon its back an inscription which urged him "to love Boston, the place of his birth, and where his mother found the best and most sympathetic friends." Yet for some obscure reason an antipathy to that place began early to show itself, for though his first volume of poems (1827) bore upon its title page the legend "By a Bostonian" he nevertheless omitted to mention the place of his birth both in the letter of biographical facts which he wrote to his brother in 1835 and in the sketch of his life (full of deliberate falsehood) which he supplied to James Russell Lowell in 1845. Loving to call himself a Virginian, he resented the accident that caused him to be born in the New England city, and it is possible also that he made in childhood a connection between that city and the humiliating circumstance of his origin. We know that his schoolfellows taunted him with being the son of an actress, and it may be that in receiving those first wounds of the spirit he identified the place of his birth with its heritage of shame, but whatever was the nucleus of his irrational dislike it soon gathered about it a complex of ideas all hateful and despicable.

His fear of his own too great tendency toward irrational fancies led him to a hatred of transcendentalism in all its branches. Carlyle to him was "an ass" and Emerson and Marguaret Fuller were merely imitators of Carlyle's manner; Boston was the American home of transcendentalism and so the two hatreds strengthened and reinforced one another. Moreover, Poe, as the representative of Southern letters, grew jealous of New

England as the center of literary life, he envied the prosperity, fame, and happiness of the Boston group and he was drawn into a bitter attack upon Longfellow. Thus all his misfortunes and all his hatred seemed to focus there. Of the reasons with all their ramifications he was probably but dimly conscious but the very name conjured up in him a blind fury. His malady made him accept his various emotions as the ultimate reality without, in many cases, comprehending their roots, and hence this fury seemed reasonable and righteous. Boston, the center of all evil, deserved no quarter and no consideration. It and its inhabitants were outside the pale and everything done to them was deserved and justifiable. In dealing with such people and such a city one forgets one's gentleness and gentility as one forgets it in struggling with a beast or scotching a snake.

From the effects of such a psychological process no one is wholly free. Given a prejudice rooted deeply enough in the unconsciousness no man has a reasonableness or a sense of justice capable of restraining it, but one of the measures of sanity is the degree of one's freedom from such uncontrollable obsessions. Poe, who lived upon his complexes and whose neurotic adjustment to an intolerable set of circumstances depended upon his ability to believe in a rational basis for the peculiar twists of his mind, was, as a result, completely at their mercy, since to understand his own mental processes would be to destroy the protection against reality which it was their function to give. The natural foundation of his character was honest, kindly, and gentle and if he seemed on occasion to contradict this character it was because he could not see a given reality clearly enough to be able to judge of his own actions.

Such, in all probability, is the explanation of his conduct not only in the Boston affair but at various other moments in his life which are so puzzling and so distressing to those who wish wholly to justify him without admitting the streak of madness which runs through both him and his work. Certainly a similar psychological process will serve to explain both the plagiarism of his *Conchologist's First Book* and the apparently unmotivated violence of his attack upon Longfellow.

The first of these incidents is worth but the briefest mention. The book in question, intended as a textbook for schools, appeared as by Poe and was copyrighted in his name in 1839 in spite of the fact that it was entirely a compilation upon a subject of which the alleged author knew nothing and in places was closely paraphrased or directly copied from other books to which no credit was given. In his own day Poe was severely criticised for his part in this dishonest transaction and since then it has been variously excused, but the fact seems to be that it was the result partly of a concatenation of circumstances, partly of that species of blindness of which we have just spoken. Shortly before, Harper and Brothers had published an elaborate and expensive *Manual of Conchology* by Thomas Wyatt which had failed to sell. Wyatt was anxious to reap the benefits of a cheaper edition without destroying such sale as the original book might have and he arranged with another publisher to have a volume based upon it issued under another name. Poe, as a needy hack, accepted the job and with the flair for a hoax which he had so perfectly utilized in his fiction he took advantage of the opportunity offered to appear as a man of scientific learning, writing an introduction which is closely paraphrased from another book upon the subject, copying the plates from this same volume, printing a chapter *Explanation of the Parts of Shells* which is taken verbatim and without any acknowledgment from the same source and making up the rest of the book by basing it, apparently with the permission of the author but again without acknowledgment, upon the Wyatt book.

When the Philadelphia *Saturday Evening Post* accused him of plagiarism he wrote an indignant letter in which he calls the charge wholly false, says that the work was written "in conjunction with Professor Thomas Wyatt, and Professor McMurtrie of Philadelphia—my name being put to the work as best known and most likely to add to its circulation," and declaring that he "wrote the preface and Introduction" but failing to acknowledge that the substance of this introduction is taken from another. Doubtless Poe's poverty had something to do with his lending his name for use in this way, but even in the letter just referred to a certain apparent disingenuousness is evident and one cannot escape the impression that he was willing to accept complacently the credit for knowledge which he did not have and works of which he was not in any true sense the author. Poe played, as I have said before, at being a scientist but he was in fact so little of one that he hardly realized the gulf which lies between a scientist and a compiler. He could speak of this book as being written "in conjunction" with two reputable professors without being entirely aware of the sorry rôle he played or quite knowing that he did not have the competence which he liked to believe that he possessed. Yet at the same time he was ready enough to accuse others of peculations similar to his own. Plagiarism was one of his manias, and just as, in the manner described in a previous chapter, he ridiculed others for stealing their learning from Disraeli at the very moment almost when he was doing it himself, so too he was capable of writing on the subject of other compilers in the following strain:

"It is the practice of quacks to paraphrase page after page, rearranging the order of paragraphs, making a slight alteration in point of fact here and there, but preserving the spirit of the whole, its information, erudition etc. etc., while everything is so *rewritten* as to leave no room for the direct charge of plagiarism; and this is considered and lauded as originality. Now, he who, in availing himself of the labors of his predecessors (and it is clear that all scholars *must* avail themselves of such labors)—he who shall copy *verbatim* the passages to be desired, without attempt at palming off their spirit as original with himself, is certainly no plagiarist, even if he fail to make *direct* acknowledgment of indebtedness—is unquestionably *less* of the plagiarist than the disingenuous and contemptible quack who wriggles himself, as above explained, into a reputation for originality, a reputation quite out of place in a case of this kind— the public, of course, never caring a straw whether he be original or not."

Poe was guilty of both the greater and the lesser plagiarisms as they are here defined, and yet it is doubtful if there was in it any wholly conscious hypocrisy.

Poe's great gift was, as has been indicated before, the gift of rationalization. He knew from direct experience what the method of the plagiarist was but he could turn that knowledge against others while at the same time he was able to explain away his own guilt in a manner which was, at least to himself, entirely satisfactory.

Many factors contributed also to produce the bitterness of his attack upon Longfellow. There is, of course, no reason to suppose that he did not have a genuine perception of the weaknesses of the latter's art but it must be remembered that he did not always have the horror of the sentimental and the maudlin which has so much to do with the present distaste for Longfellow. For Tom Moore and Mrs. Browning he expressed the most extravagant admiration. Tennyson he thought "the noblest poet who ever lived"; for the various feeble female songstresses of his generation he had so infatuated a regard that "the genius of Miss Landon" made her almost unequalled in *the passionate purity* of her verse, and upon one occasion he was led to exclaim: "Hemans, Baillie, Landon, and, loveliest of all, Norton! . . . France with her gaiety; Italy with her splendid genius; even Greece with her passionate enthusiasm, cannot rival such a galaxy. And this glory, too, belongs wholly to the present century; for though the harp of England has often been struck by female hands, it has heretofore only seldom given forth the rare, deep, prolonged harmony which now rolls from its chords." Surely, then, a purity of literary taste was not alone responsible for the attack upon the most popular of American poets.

As far back as 1839 Poe had given *Hyperion* the

bluntly unfavorable reception that it deserved and when in 1840 he reviewed *Voices of the Night* he set himself against the growing fame of the author by remarking, after bestowing some praise, that Longfellow "appears to us singularly deficient in all those important faculties which give artistic power, and without which never was immortality affected" and by accusing him with some show of reason of copying his *Midnight Mass for the Dying Year* from Tennyson's *The Death of the Old Year*. In 1841 he wrote to Rufus Griswold, then engaged in compiling his *The Poets and Poetry of America*, with the intention of recommending himself for inclusion in the volume, and in the course of the letter accused Longfellow of stealing the poem *The Beleaguered City* from Poe's own *Haunted Palace*.

It was probably at this moment that his conception of Longfellow as a plagiarist crystalized. He was conscious of the fact that the New Englander's fame was greater than his merits justified, he was ever more keenly aware of the fact that his own fame, beside that of Longfellow, was pitifully and undeservedly small, and he needed only the perception of a fancied resemblance between two poems to set the sense of wrong which he always had to burning with a feverish heat. The plagiarist, he said on a later occasion when defending his charge, generally "pilfers from some poverty-stricken, and therefore neglected man of genius, on the reasonable supposition that this neglected man of genius will very soon cut his throat, or die of starvation (the sooner the better, no doubt,) and that in the meantime he will be too busy in keeping the wolf from the door to look after the purloiners of his property—and too poor, and too cowed, and for these reasons too contemptible, under any circumstances, to dare accuse of so base a thing as theft, the wealthy and triumphant gentleman of elegant leisure who has only done the vagabond too much honor in knocking him down and robbing him upon the highway." There can be no doubt that in writing thus Poe was picturing himself as the victim of the fortunate New Englander.

Now Longfellow, in a letter to Griswold, denied that he had ever seen Poe's poem until long after his own was written; there is indeed little resemblance between the two, and Longfellow, whatever his deficiencies as a poet, was a painfully honest man who would certainly not lie upon such a matter, but Poe, suffering both from real and fancied wrongs, was perfectly convinced that his more successful rival for popular fame was a deliberate thief and from then on he never spared him. In a brief article published in 1841 he accused him in general of "imitation verging upon downright theft," and when in 1845 a letter signed Outis appeared in a New York paper protesting against Poe's charges of plagiarism he was stung as he was always stung by the least hint of contradiction into voluminous, complicated, and occasionally violent controversy. Briggs, editor of the *Broadway Journal*, wrote to Lowell: "Poe is a monomaniac on the subject of plagiarism, and I thought it best to allow him to ride his hobby to death in the outset and be done with it."

In a series of five articles in the *Broadway Journal* Poe now defended his charges against Longfellow and others and accused the former of two new crimes—first, of palming off a close copy of a ballad by Motherwell as a translation from the German and, second, of stealing a scene from Poe's fragment *Politian* for his own drama *The Spanish Student*. To the first of these charges, which did not originate with Poe, there was some ap-- parent foundation, for, as Longfellow afterwards explained, he had in good faith translated a German translation of the poem in question without being aware of its origin, but to the second there was no foundation whatever since the two are alike in nothing except that both embody various conventional touches of the closet drama. But by this time Poe was beyond reason and to the end of his life he believed Longfellow to be *d* man "a little quacky *per se*" as he called him in *The Literati* and hence to be insulted along with the other New Englanders upon the occasion of the famous reading.

From all the controversy the chief object of attack remained almost wholly aloof, but in 1849 he did write a letter to *The Southern Literary Messenger* which contains one sentence revealing a flash of remarkably penetrating insight. "The harshness of his criticisms," writes Longfellow, "I have never attributed to anything but the irritation of a sensitive nature chafed by some indefinite sense of wrong" and the remark is, as far as it goes, as penetrating as any which any contemporary ever made, for it strikes with its hypothetised "indefinite sense of wrong" not only at the root cause of Poe's attack upon Longfellow but àt the root of his whole mental process as well, in spite of the fact that the sense of wrong went back into regions of the mind and character of which the man who gave the explanation was totally ignorant. Poe's attitude toward the New England poet was not justified but neither was it consciously malicious. His was that egotism of suffering which makes every man in pain

POE'S COTTAGE AT FORDHAM

From a photograph

center the whole world about himself and he struck out with that blind rage which suffering inspires. When one is sure of agony one is likely to attribute it to the person nearest at hand.

In the course of the next section of the present work I shall have occasion to mention one or two other disgracefully intemperate quarrels into which the violence of Poe's temper plunged him, but it will be as well in rounding out the present sketch of his public life during the middle period to say something of his most fateful relationship with the outside world—his friendship or enmity (he himself evidently did not know which it was) with his literary executor, Griswold. There can be no question of reversing the general verdict which assigns the villain's part to the "false friend" who accepted the task of editing Poe's work in order to villify him but there are sufficient evidences in the story of Poe's peculiar instability and irrationality of behavior to make it worth while to regard it dispassionately.

The Rev. Rufus Wilmot Griswold, whose published diary and correspondence sufficiently reveal his character, was, to begin with, the last man in the world with whom Poe was likely to have anything in common. The son of a pious Vermont farmer and of a mother who wrote him when was twenty-three years old, "Rufus, are you a Christian, are you prepared to meet your God?", he became a minister and took up literature as an adjunct to piety. By no means a fool but thoroughly a provincial he had encyclopedic knowledge of the polite minor literature of America and a gift for clear not unforceful writing but his taste was for the pseudo-classic and conventional. In his correspondence he speaks of such men as Pope and Goldsmith "whom I preferred to the romantic and passionate school" and he was the last man in the world genuinely to appreciate Poe's art or to forgive him his vagaries.

It was apparently in the office of *Graham's Magazine*, of which Poe was one of the editors, that the two first met. Graham always spoke of Poe in the friendliest manner, but the exact cause of the termination of the latter's editorship of the magazine is not known, though it is evident that Poe was never thoroughly happy there in spite of the fact that the magazine was the most famous and prosperous of which he had ever had charge. He speaks of Graham as a "very gentlemanly although an exceedingly weak man" for whom he had no "especial respect," and he was, according to another member of the editorial staff, always discontented with his position of subordination to Graham. It seems that upon one occasion Poe had been absent for several days from some cause, probably intemperance, and that when he returned he found Griswold seated in his chair. Conscious, doubtless, of his own dereliction he seems to have leaped to the conclusion that he had been summarily displaced and with the quick anger of wounded dignity characteristic of him he turned upon his heel and left the office without a word of explanation. From this moment he centered upon Griswold, as he had centered upon Longfellow, the hatred of the world in general which his sense of wrong inspired but he continued to behave towards Griswold in a manner bafflingly ambiguous.

It was in the spring of 1842 that Poe severed his relations with *Graham's,* and in the following year he published in the *Philadelphia Saturday Museum* a long anonymous review of Griswold's *Poets and Poetry of America* in the course of which he not only roundly damned the book but indulged in elaborate ridicule of the author and expressed the following opinion of him as an editor: "The review department of 'Graham's Magazine,' and its original literary contents, monthly, exhibit ample evidence of his want of taste and inability if not of critical honesty; while its very cover displays his want of judgment in commonsense business matters, and his egotism and petty envy and dislike of men he *dares* not openly assail." Later he delivered in Philadelphia a lecture marked by another violent attack upon the same man and yet in February 1845 he was writing to Griswold in the friendliest possible manner and adding the following postcript: "I presume you understand that in the repetition of my lecture on the Poets (in N. Y.) I left out *all* that was offensive to yourself?" Still later, it appears, he was attempting to borrow money.

The details of the story here outlined are confused and controverted. If one wishes to accept as genuine the letters which Griswold published as having come from Poe, then the latter appears in a still worse light; and if one wishes to accept the story told many years later by Thomas Dunn English then the affair takes on a resemblance to that of the Boston reading, for, according to English, Poe accepted from Griswold a commission to review his book, took the money for it, and then gloried in the fine joke which he had played in making the review so slashing that it could not in all probability be used. The truth seems to be that the review in question was mildly favorable though not enthusiastic enough to suit Griswold; but even if one prefers to reject all this as mere fabrication on the part of Griswold and his friends the facts stated above are proved by unassailable documents and clearly reveal enough to convict Poe of petty malice and actual insincerity. Having indulged in violently personal attacks upon Griswold at a time when, so far as we know, Poe had nothing against him except the irrational enmity born of the scene in Graham's office, he later attempted to make up the quarrel when he thought Griswold might be of use to him and by cancelling his remarks in the lecture practically admitted that they had been inspired by anger alone.

There is no need to defend Griswold's conduct. It is evident from a letter written by Briggs during his lifetime that Griswold was spreading scandal about Poe and after Poe's death Griswold wrote in a letter to Mrs. Whitman "I was not his friend, nor was he mine," so that it is pretty evident that the amicability revealed in their letters to one another was pure pretense. Moreover the famous death notice which he wrote in the *Tribune* was full of misstatement intended to damage Poe and it appears that in the controversy which arose over it he tampered with the text of Poe's letters. But to blacken the biographer will not wholly whitewash Poe and it is evident that in the quarrel Poe played a part which distinctly revealed the violence of his temperament and which was besides not wholly honorable in that he, before Griswold, used his position as critic to vent a purely personal spite. One is forced to conclude that Griswold far outdid Poe in malice, but it seems pretty evident that the first provocation came from Poe.

In the usual account of Poe, Griswold and alcohol

are made to play together the rôle of scapegoat. Griswold's conduct, painted in the darkest possible colors,
and declaimed against with righteous rhetoric, serves
to distract attention from Poe's own shortcomings,
while alcohol, our national bugaboo, is made responsible
for whatever other eccentricities or shortcomings cannot
be otherwise explained away. To employ such technique
is to obtain the nearest possible approach to success in
the attempt to make of Poe a figure easily assimilable into
the popular tradition of the lovable though wayward and
neglected genius, but because those who employ it cannot
fairly take account of all the available facts they have
never been able to present a wholly consistent picture or
to make him quite comprehensible. Most people, it appears, find it painful to admit that a genius is not necessarily a gentleman, but when facts are as clear as in Poe's
case they are it seems hardly worth while to distort them.
He was certainly quite capable of himself provoking the
quarrels from which he suffered.

VII

In 1845 Poe reached the height of his fame. After the severance of his connection with *Graham's Magazine* he had lingered on in Philadelphia for some time and made many contributions to the same periodical, but in April 1844 he had taken up his residence for the second time in New York and his various claims upon public attention began to consolidate themselves. His three early volumes of verse had attracted little attention and his voluminous writings had been too scattered to take immediate effect, but under his management *Graham's* had become perhaps the most important magazine in America and the first edition of collected stories, the two volumes of *Tales of the Grotesque and Arabesque*, had been published in Philadelphia in 1840 and followed by Number One (all published) of *The Prose Romances of Edgar A. Poe*, in 1843. His hoax on the subject of mesmerism, *The Facts in the Case of M. Valdemar*, had caused considerable talk in England, *The Murders in the Rue Morgue* had been translated and discussed in French journals, Irving had praised him, and Lowell in a private letter had called him "almost the only *fearless* American critic." Now however the publication of *The Raven* in January 1845 first scattered his fame far and wide and made him from then on a marked man.

There is, indeed, some reason for believing that Poe recognized the potential popularity of the poem and that he deliberately used it as a bid for fame. He was not above a little puffery, for as far back as 1829 he had twisted a contemptuous newspaper critique into what appeared to be praise and in his anonymous attack upon Griswold he had incorporated some self-addressed compliments to himself. Now when *The Raven* was first published in the New York *Evening Mirror* he wrote a long laudatory note signed "Quarles" to accompany the poem and to point out its excellences which included, among other things, "one of the most felicitous specimens of unique rhyming which has for some time met our eye." He also wrote to *The Southern Literary Messenger* requesting the editor "to suspend the well known rule of the *Messenger* against republications, to take out the middle dividing line of its page and let the poem appear in full in the beautiful typography of the *Messenger*." Poe did not himself regard *The Raven* as artistically the best of his poems, and there is a certain mechanical air about it which suggests that the element of calculation which he boasted of as the essential factor in composition did enter to a larger degree in the making of this poem than in his better work, but whether or not its great success was the result of a deliberately planned sensation that success was complete.

Reprinted in a number of magazines, it leaped into an immediate popularity and quickly spread to other countries. From England, Elizabeth Barrett wrote: "Your 'Raven' has produced a sensation, a 'fit o' horror', here in England. Some of my friends are taken by the fear of it and some by the music. I hear of persons haunted by the 'Nevermore,' and one acquaintance of mine who has the misfortune of possessing a 'bust of

Pallas' can never bear to look at it in the twilight. I think you will like to be told our great poet Mr. Browning, the author of 'Paracelsus' and the 'Bells and Pomgranates,' was struck much by the rhythm of that poem." In America Poe was often called upon to deliver it, and the manner in which he did so has been thus recalled by one who heard him: "He would turn down the lamps till the room was almost dark, then standing in the center of the apartment he would recite those wonderful lines in the most melodious of voices; gradually becoming more and more enthused with his new creation, he forgot time, spectators, his personal identity, as the wild hopes and repressed longings of his heart found vent in the impassioned words of the poem. To the listeners came the sounds of falling rain and waving branches; the Raven flapped his dusky wings above the bust of Pallas, and the lovely face of Lenore appeared to rise before them. So marvelous was his power as a reader that the auditors would be afraid to draw breath lest the enchanted spell be broken." Most of those who heard him seem to have been greatly impressed, but to modern taste it would probably seem, as Professor Gildersleeve remembers that it seemed to him, a little bit overdone. Poe was tasting for the first time to the full the sound of actual, audible applause.

The effect of the wide-spread popularity of this poem in consolidating his fame was immediately evident. The year in which it appeared saw the publication in New York of *The Raven and Other Poems* as well as a volume of *Tales by Edgar A. Poe*. About the same time he began to receive tributes of praise from other writers. In 1846 he received complimentary letters from Hawthorne, William Gilmore Simms and John Pendleton Cooke, in England the *Literary Gazette* contained a favorable review of his tales which was copied in *The Living Age*, and yet his position was not nearly so comfortable as one might suppose, for this reputation brought but little money and he was still desperately poor.

Then, as now, little was to be made by the mere free lance contributor to magazines. The most distinguished of his contemporaries had sources of income other than their writings—Longfellow and Lowell became professors; Irving, Prescott, Motley, Bancroft and Bayard Taylor were made foreign ministers; Hawthorne was the incumbent of government positions—and for the writer who depended upon writing alone only an editorial position could make life possible. But Poe, though he had no difficulty in obtaining such positions, could never hold one long and was often dependent upon the miserable sums which he received for his work to keep him alive. He had previously repeatedly failed to interest publishers in a collected edition of the tales, and in a letter written in 1845 he speaks of his hope of getting sixty dollars more than the one hundred and twenty-five which he has already collected as the proceeds from both the volume of poems and the volume of stories published in that year; for *The Bells* he got forty-five dollars— a remarkably high price—and for *The Poetic Principle* thirty dollars, from the consideration of which sums it will be evident why he engaged in constant effort to effect loans which he did not always pay back.

If, indeed, there was any change in his financial status, it became more desperate as his fame increased. In 1844 he had obtained a very minor position as a "mechani-

cal paragraphist" on the New York *Evening Mirror*
and in 1845 he became assistant and then sole editor
and proprietor of the *Broadway Journal,* but under his
management this paper mysteriously expired at the beginning of the following year and at no time did he
escape from the direst necessity.   In May 1845 he wrote
to a friend: "For the last three or four months I have
been working 14 or 15 hours a day—and yet, Thomas,
I have made no money.   I am as poor now as ever 1
was in my life—except in hope, which is by no means
bankable."   Early in 1847 friends were compelled to
raise about a hundred dollars to defray the expenses
of Virginia's illness and the same desperate state of
affairs continued up to the very moment of Poe's death,
for in August 1849 Mrs. Clemm was compelled to write
to Griswold—of all people—in the following strain: "I
feel that you will pardon the liberty I take in addressing
you, but the extreme urgency of my situation compels
me to do so.   Mr. Poe has been absent from home
for some weeks; he is now in Richmond and has been
very ill, and unable to send me any money since he left,
and is much distressed for fear of my suffering.   Indeed I *have suffered.*   I have been very sick, and entirely
unable to make the least exertion.   I have been without
the necessaries of life for many days, and would not
apply to anyone, in hopes that I would soon receive
some aid from my poor Eddy.   He writes me that he
is getting better, and hopes he will soon be able to
attend to business.   I confide in you, dear sir, and beg
you to loan me a small sum until I can receive some
from him.   I have not the means to go to the city, but
a note addressed to Mrs. Maria Clemm, care of E. A.

Poe, New York will reach me. A gentleman in the neighborhood asks every day for me at the post office."

That a man whose fame was no longer confined even to his own country should be perpetually in such desperate straights may, at first sight, seem strange even when his own irregular habits and the difficult position of any imaginative writer are considered, but it must be remembered that Poe did not at any time win any really warm admiration from his contemporaries. His power and originality wrung from them an unwilling respect but he never either asked for or received more. His success was, as he wished it to be, a success of scandal, for he had no love for the human race and he desired from it only the recognition which fear inspires. He openly flouted the moralistic conception of literature which was almost universally held and he gave clear indication that he set no store whatever by those kindly and sentimental virtues which the society in which he lived had elevated to a position of supreme importance. People did not really like his stories; editors often refused to accept them and did not print them except unwillingly. Critics, even while they praised his genius, made no bones of the fact that they did not approve.

As far back as 1839 a correspondent had written him as follows: "I am sure you will appreciate my candor when I say that I never could feel much interest in that class of compositions. I mean that I never could experience pleasure in reading tales of horror and mystery however much the narrative should be dignified by genius. They leave a painful and melancholy impression on my mind, and I do not perceive their tendency to improve the heart." Many a time afterward Poe was compelled to listen to similar opinions, and in the last phrase especially is stated the insuperable objection found by the great body of Poe's readers to his work. Even the article written in 1846 by M. F. Tupper and copied from the London *Literary Gazette* by *The Living Age* added the inevitable qualifications to its praise by condemning "such a tale as 'The Black Cat,' which is impossible and revolting," "such an argument as 'Mesmeric Revelation,' which attempts too daring a solution of that deepest of riddles, the nature of the Deity, and such a juvenile production [!] as 'The Fall of the House of Usher.'" Poe nowhere specifically rejects the morality of his times, he may not indeed have realized how completely he did in his heart reject it, but its influence is absent from his work and his contemporaries correctly recognized him as a spiritual outcast from his age.

Four years after his death Richard Stoddard wrote of him in the *National Magazine* and expressed the current opinion of his works. "The school of literature to which Poe belongs," wrote Stoddard, "and of which he is certainly the master, is one we thoroughly dislike. . . . It mercilessly exposes the depths and secrets of the heart, laying bare to the eyes all what but a few are strong enough to survey unharmed—the black gulfs and chasms of our spiritual nature. It leagues itself with darkness generally, reversing the very life and mission of all literature and art, viz: the promotion of joy and gladness, and undying faith in the good and beautiful. What we want is not darkness but light; not thorns in our path, but roses, and everywhere dew and freshness. The literature which does not give us this and does not make us happier and better is not true and good, but, in spite of its beauty and sublimity, false and pernicious."

It must be remembered also that Poe's personal relations with his public were such as to confirm the fear and distaste which his works inspired. He demanded admiration, he dared people not to give it to him, but he never sought to flatter, to intrigue, or even to compromise. He signalized his arrival in New York by the publication in the New York *Sun* of the famous *Balloon Hoax*, a fantastic account of the alleged arrival in Charleston of a trans-Atlantic balloon, and then laughed heartily when, incredible as it may seem, at least a portion of the public swallowed the tale as sober fact. But the player of practical jokes, whatever sensation he may arouse, does not endear himself to his victims and the same may be said of a man who writes as Poe did in the *Literati* series which ran through six numbers of *Godey's Lady's Book* in 1846. These sketches, reckless in praise and censure, created another sensation but they did not increase the respect which conventional people had for him.

Indeed to say that Poe was famous, even after the publication of *The Raven*, is to be not quite accurate; notorious is a word which serves better both to describe his actual position and to explain why it was that while all spoke of him few were concerned to know into what desperate shipwreck his life was drifting. "I have sometimes amused myself," he wrote in *Marginalia*, "by endeavoring to fancy what would be the fate of an individual gifted, or rather accursed with an intellect *very* far superior to that of his race. Of course he would be conscious of his own superiority; nor could he (if otherwise constituted as man is) help manifesting his consciousness. Thus he would make himself enemies at all points. And since his opinions and speculations would widely differ from those of *all* mankind—that he would be considered a madman, is evident. How horribly painful such a condition! Hell could invent no greater torture than that of a being charged with abnormal weakness on account of being abnormally strong." Poe was, of course, thinking of himself. Because of his sense of superiority, raised by his neurosis to a far greater height than his actual powers would have made legitimate, he felt himself a superman forced to dwell among pygmies and it was impossible for him to reveal anything except scorn for this race of men whose admiration he had to have at the same time that he despised them.

Doubtless he was at times completely beside himself through madness complicated with intoxication, as the following story told by Richard Henry Stoddard in his *Recollections* will indicate. It seems that as a young man Stoddard, who came afterwards to hate Poe but concerning whose veracity in a matter of straight fact there is no reason to doubt, had sent to Poe a poem and received the promise that it would appear the following week. Instead appeared a notice to the effect that the editor believed the poem to be a plagiarism and would not publish it unless assured of its authenticity. Stoddard went to the office and found Poe asleep in his chair: "'What do you want?' he snapped out. 'I have come Mr. Poe, to assure you of the authenticity of the Ode on a Grecian Flute.' He glared at me, and without waiting to hear what I had to say, declared that I was a liar, and consigned me to perdition. Then he rose surlily and threatened to kick me out of the office if I did not get out at once; which I did."

With people too unimportant or too weak to arouse his envy he could sometimes remain upon friendly terms but it is worthy to note that with the possible exception of Graham and Willis every man capable of really aiding him was somehow alienated. He began, for example, on the friendliest terms with Lowell, but he could not bear to be friends with a man who had won so much praise as Lowell, and soon he was denouncing him in the most violent terms, ostensibly for being an abolitionist, but actually because Lowell was receiving too much of the praise which Poe could not bear to see bestowed upon anyone other than himself.

"No Southerner," he wrote, "who does not wish to be insulted, and at the same time revolted by a bigotry the most obstinately blind and deaf, should ever touch a volume by this author. His fanaticism about slavery is a mere local outbreak of the same innate wrong-headedness which, if he owned slaves, would manifest itself in the atrocious ill-treatment of them, with the murder of any abolitionist who should endeavor to set them free. A fanatic of Mr. Lowell's species is simply a fanatic for the sake of fanaticism, and must be a fanatic in whatever circumstances you place him. . . . All whom he praises are Bostonians. Other writers are barbarians, and satirized accordingly, if mentioned at all."

Lowell, like Longfellow, preferred to be magnanimous and to leave the quarrel one-sided but whenever Poe met a man like Briggs, who had been owner of the *Broadway Journal* when Poe was first employed there and hence his superior, a disgraceful battle of billingsgate was sure to result. One of his quarrels, that with Thomas Dunn English, actually reached the point of a lawsuit and Poe received damages to the extent of $250. It was probably with this money that he bought the cottage at Fordham, and the fact is not without its significance. The only money in excess of the immediate needs of the moment which Poe ever received came to him not as a tribute to the value of his services or the admiration in which he was held but as the direct result of the intensity of the hatred which he could inspire.

It has often been said that he was "misunderstood" by his contemporaries and the word is, of course, susceptible of various interpretations, but the truth is that in one sense at least, these contemporaries understood him all too well. They were, to be sure, wrong in the absurd definition of the purpose of literature which Stoddard expressed for them and hence wrong in their evaluation of Poe's work; they were provincially ignorant in their demand that a genius should be also a gentleman, but if they disliked him and his writings it was not because they failed to judge properly of either the facts of his character or the tendency of his works. They knew both the man and the literature with which they had to deal and they liked neither. They could not help listening and, in a way, admiring, but their attention was not approval and they felt no obligation toward one who never for an instant regarded himself as the servant of the public.

The generation which arose after his death greatly oversentimentalized his story, but the error of his contemporaries was exactly the reverse. They felt no shame for having neglected him because they felt him to be essentially of the devil's party, and when they did not hate him they were ready to treat his fate with the same jocose levity with which the squire treats the village drunkard. Thus Horace Greeley says in his *Recollections* that a "gushing youth" once wrote him to ask if he did not possess one of Poe's autographs and that he responded as follows: "Among my literary treasures there happens to be exactly *one* autograph of our country's lamented poet, Edgar A. Poe. It is his note of hand for fifty dollars, with my endorsement across the back. It cost me exactly $50.75 (including protest) and you may have it for half that amount." "That autograph," Greeley adds, "I regret to say remains on my hands, and is still for sale at first cost, despite the lapse of time and the depreciation of our currency." In similar vein Richard Henry Stoddard, hearing of the proposal to erect a monument to Poe in Baltimore, jocosely said that the poet had asked for bread and received a (tomb)stone, and the same man tells with vast delight and a complete absence of any sense of the cruel irony involved that he had made seven hundred dollars (about four times the total proceeds of Poe's *Tales* and *The Raven and other Poems*) from the sale in various forms of one anecdote about the unfortunate genius. "Do I blame Poe?" he writes elsewhere. "The gods forbid! With a race of hardy New England sailors behind me, and behind him a stock of hard drinking Marylanders, his father an inefficient player, and his mother a fairly good English actress and vocalist, who am I, pray, that I should censure anybody?" Thoroughly protected by such self-righteousness, it was not likely that many of Poe's contemporaries would feel themselves much troubled about him.

Thus it was that his increasing notoriety brought him no outward advantage except the extremely doubtful one of an entrée into the second-rate literary salons of New York. From 1845 on Poe was much in literary society though Virginia was seldom with him. In the salons of the very minor poetess, Charlotte Lynch (Mrs. Botta), of Dr. Dewey, and others of their kind Poe was given the privilege of mingling with a predominately feminine society of the solemn near great. William Cullen Bryant, Fitz-Green Halleck, Rufus Griswold, and G. P. Morris, author of *Woodman Spare that Tree*, were the most distinguished of the people he sometimes met, but these luminaries were lost among a motley crowd of lesser lights like Elizabeth Oakes Smith, Dr. Thomas Ward, author of *Passaic, A Group of Poems Touching that River*, and, in the words of Stoddard, two others of the swarming sisterhood of American singers, one "an elderly spinster who was renowned through one of her solemn lyrics, entitled, I think, 'He Came Too Late,' " the other, "a more hopeful married woman, whose songs were of a more cheerful cast." Later he was to meet Mrs. Frances S. Osgood in the same company and to intensify the bitterness between himself and Griswold by becoming the latter's rival for the affections of this poetic lady.

During the season of 1845–46 Poe was, in the words of a letter written by one who was also a frequenter of these salons, "the observed of all observers." He never, it appears, refused a request to "deliver *The Raven*," and that elaborate courtesy combined with the most high-

flown Southern deference to "the ladies" which was characteristic of him in his sane moments made him the idol
of all the female hearts. Through the eyes of observers
we may see him surrounded by an admiring group de-
molishing the lofty Bostonian opinions of Margaret
Fuller or uttering profound dicta with a manner of
grand detachment.

"As a conversationalist we do not remember his equal,"
says Mrs. Whitman, in whom, since she had completely
lost her head in a romantic infatuation with Poe, we may
pardon some exaggeration. "We have heard the veteran
Landor (called by high authority the best talker in
England) discuss with scathing sarcasm the popular
writers of the day, convey his political animosities by
fierce invectives on the 'pretentious coxcomb Albert' and
'the cunning knave Napoleon,' or describe, in words of
strange depths and tenderness, the peerless charms of
goodness, and the *naïve* social graces in the beautiful
mistress of Gore House, 'the most gorgeous Lady Bless-
ington.' We have heard Howadji talk of the gardens
of Damascus till the air seemed purpled and perfumed
with its roses. We have listened to the trenchant and
vivid talk of the Autocrat; to the brilliant and exhaust-
less colloquial resources of John Neal and Margaret
Fuller. We have heard the racy talk of Orestes Brown-
son in the old days of freedom and power, have listened
to the serene wisdom of Alcott, and treasured up
memorable sentences from the golden lips of Emerson.
Unlike the conversational power evinced by any of these,
was the earnest, opulent, unpremeditated speech of
Edgar Poe. Like his writings, it presented a combination
of qualities rarely met with in the same person,—a cool,

decisive judgment, a wholly unconventional courtesy and a sincere grace of manner, and an imperious enthusiasm, which brought all hearers within the circle of its influence."

We must not, however, suppose that even during this brief period when Poe was for the first and only time of his life an accepted member of any society he had ceased to be somewhat sinister. Soon scandal was to break over him and to divide his acquaintances into two violently acrimonious parties. He was not really a member of this group and people were uneasily if faintly aware of the fact. J. M. Daniel, United States Minister at Turin, noted his curious detachment and fell to a large extent under the spell of his mysterious manner. "In his animated moods," says Daniel, "he talked with an abstracted earnestness, as if he were dictating to an amanuensis; and, if he spoke of individuals, his ideas ran upon their moral and intellectual qualities, rather than upon the idiosyncrasies of their active, visible phenomena, or the peculiarities of their manner. . . . His proud reserve, his profound melancholy, his unworldliness—may we not say his *unearthliness*—of nature made his character one very difficult of comprehension, to the casual observer. The complexity of his intellect, its incalculable resources, and his masterly control of these resources when brought into requisition for the illustration of some favorite theme or cherished creation, led to the current belief that its action was purely arbitrary, that he could write without emotion or earnestness at the deliberate dictation of the will."

Thus it is evident that Poe was succeeding in his effort to impose his legend of himself upon others, but it was a dangerous legend, and the greater his success the more precarious his position in a society which, thoroughly conventional, wished merely to play safely with imitation literature. Even at the very height of his social success another writer remarks in a letter dated January 7, 1846: "People seem to think there is something uncanny about him, and the weirdest stories are told and, what is more, *believed*, about his mesmeric experiences, at the mention of which he always smiles. His smile is captivating!—Everybody wants to know him; but only a few people seem to get well acquainted with him."

Doubtless Poe enjoyed his experiences, for the smell of that incense for which he had longed was at last directly sensible in his nostrils. Yet it was, for him, by no means healthful. It intensified while it gratified his mania for deference and, worse yet, it stirred in him the most fatal of his psychic forces—the strangely baffled erotic impulse. Women like Mrs. Osgood and Mrs. Whitman played with fire under the guise of sentimental and poetic affection, their "nobility" and "purity" disguised from Poe the danger until it was too late, and his relations with them led the way to the final catastrophe which was precipitated in part by the fact that he lost the grip which he had been compelled to hold through life upon his amorous nature. Moreover, he was now compelled to live in three worlds instead of two, for the contrast which had always existed between his inward and outward life was hardly greater than the contrast between the mock grandeur of the salon and his actual private situation.

It was during this same significant year, 1846, that he

moved to the little cottage in the open fields near Fordham, and when he embarked at New York upon the train which was to deposit him near his lonely dwelling it must have been more difficult than ever to retain any grip upon reality. What, indeed, was he? The master of the gloomily magnificent House of Usher, and the recipient of strange mesmeric experiences? A fashionable literary lion and squire of Dames? Or merely a beaten hack who had already exhausted most of the possibilities of borrowing which had kept him alive? As he sat by the bed of his now dying wife, while Mrs. Clemm hovered protectingly in the background, he sought often to reduce his experiences, his emotions, and his desires to some sort of order but instead the chaos became madder and madder.

About the little cottage there was, as observers have described it to us, a deceptive air of peace. It was spotlessly neat. A cherry tree bloomed near the door and the grass which surrounded it was broken by beds of heliotrope and mignonette, but as the fall of 1846 came on the dire poverty of the inhabitants resulted in actual physical suffering that grew more and more intense as Poe drifted further and further towards unmistakable insanity. In December 1846 Mrs. M. E. Hewitt wrote to Mrs. Osgood: "The Poes are in the same state of physical and pecuniary suffering—indeed worse, than they were last summer, for now the cold weather is added to their accumulation of ills. I went to enquire of Mr. Post about them. He confirmed all that I had previously heard of their condition. Although he says that Mrs. Clemm has never told him they were in want, yet she borrows a shilling often *to get a letter from the of-*

FRANCES S. OSGOOD

From an engraving

ficc—but Mrs. Gove has been to see the Poes and found them living in the greatest wretchedness. I am endeavoring to get up a contribution for them among the editors, and the matter has got into print—very much to my regret, as I fear it will hurt Poe's pride to have his affairs made so public."

Meanwhile Virginia, the keystone of the crazy structure which was Poe's life, was slowly dissolving in death. "I saw her in her bed-chamber," wrote one observer. "There was no clothing on the bed, which was only straw, but a snow-white counterpane and sheets. The weather was cold, and the sick lady had the dreadful chills that accompany the hectic fever of consumption. She lay on the straw-bed, wrapped in her husband's greatcoat, with a large tortoise-shell cat on her bosom. The wonderful cat seemed conscious of her great usefulness. The coat and the cat were the sufferer's only means of warmth; except as her husband held her hands, and her mother her feet." Thus it was that at the very moment when Poe might have seemed to an outsider to be reaching the climax of his career the inevitable catastrophe was clearly in sight.

On January 30, 1847 Virginia died. However peculiar Poe's love for her undoubtedly was, there is no question of its tenderness. For a long time he had sought to prepare himself for the inevitable, but he was plunged into frantic grief which was complicated by the beginning of the madness which her death released. His marriage to her had stood between him and insanity. She was the peg upon which he had been able to hang the elaborate rationalization of his predicament and when she was removed nothing stood between him and the full results of his malformed soul. It was only a question of time until its conflicting elements should shatter him to pieces.

No sooner had her death set him dangerously free than he began that tragically ludicrous series of hectic flirtations the excitement of which helped to hasten the final debacle. His wife no longer served to hide from him the ambiguity of his emotions, and he was completely at the mercy of women. No one knows how many were the minor affairs which he began, but sentimental attachments of considerable magnitude were developed with at least four different women, to two of whom he was actually engaged to be married. While his morbidity was rapidly growing and the determining traits of his imaginative life were coming more and more clearly to dominate his waking hours; while his fits of intemperance were coming to seem more and more like madness; and while the old feeling of vague dread was growing upon him to such an extent that he could no longer bear to be alone and demanded after he had gone to bed that Mrs. Clemm should sit beside him and stroke his brow while he indulged his wild dreams; he was attempting to save himself by a search for one who could protect him as Virginia had done from the knowledge of himself.

Just before Virginia's death he had commenced a sentimental flirtation with the very emotional poetess, Mrs. Osgood, which had reached the point of scandal and caused the lady to retire in frightened haste, and now he turned to Mrs. Shew, who nursed him through fits of absolute unconsciousness but who now, like Mrs. Osgood, fled in terror from his insane ardor. Next came Mrs. Whitman, and after her the same Miss Royster who had been his boyhood sweetheart, but in every case the affair was abortive because Poe was always held back by a force just as strong as that which drove him forward. None of these women was wholly real. They stirred in him fatally erotic inpulses but he was constrained to make of them at the same time temporary embodiments of the dream woman who haunted him. He could transfer the ardor which he felt from one to the other because all were the same and because they were imaginatively quite interchangeable. "Helen—my Helen —the Helen of a thousand dreams," he called Mrs. Whitman in reference to the name which he had bestowed in childhood upon Mrs. Stanard, and to Mrs. Osgood he addressed precisely the same lines which he had formerly published in honor of a Miss Eliza White of Richmond.

It is the affair with Mrs. Whitman which is best known to us and which reveals most clearly the impasse to which the death of Virginia had led him by bringing him face to face with the fact which his marriage had served to hide. This lady, a typical example of the American blue-stocking, was a thoroughly respectable precieuse with an itch to imitate the literary gallantries of the eighteenth century. A highly emotional widow who was accustomed, it is said, to robe herself always in the conventional white of the seeress and to carry with her the scent of ether, she was sufficiently eccentric to serve as a center about which Poe could weave his strange fancies and she was so completely driven out of her mind by his extravagant ravings that she was, in spite of the protests of friends, on the point of marrying the wreck which Poe had become. He had first seen her in the summer of 1845 when he passed through the city of Providence where she lived and had caught a glimpse of her as she wandered, as was her custom, in a stately manner through her moonlit garden but though, as he said afterwards, he immediately recognized in her a kindred soul it was not until after Virginia's death that the two actually met.

Stimulated by some flattering remarks which she heard that Poe had made concerning her Mrs. Whitman wrote in 1848 a poem in his honor and when he read it he addressed to her the following letter which clearly indicated the feverish, almost delirious, state of mind which was nearly continuous with him from this time until his death.

"I have already told you that some casual words spoken of you by ——, were the first in which I had ever heard your name mentioned. She alluded to what she called 'your eccentricities,' and hinted at 'your sorrow.' Her description of the former strangely arrested—her allusion to the latter enchained and rivetted my attention.

"She had referred to thoughts, sentiments, traits, *moods*, which I knew to be my own, but which, until that moment, I had believed to be my own solely—unshared by any human being. A profound sympathy took immediate possession of my soul. I cannot better explain to you what I felt than by saying that your unknown heart seemed to pass into my bosom—there to dwell for ever—while mine, I thought, was translated into your own.

"From that hour I loved you. Since that period I have never seen nor heard your name without a shiver, half of delight, half of anxiety.—The impression left upon my mind was that you were still a wife, and it is only within the last few months that I have been undeceived in this respect.

"For this reason I shunned your presence and even the city where you lived. You may remember that once when I passed through Providence with Mrs. Osgood I positively refused to accompany her to your house, and even provoked her into a quarrel by the obstinacy and seeming unreasonableness of my refusal. I dared neither go nor say why I could not. I dared not speak of you—much less see you. For years your name never passed my lips, while my soul drank in with delirious thirst, all that was uttered in my presence respecting you.

"The merest whisper that concerned you awoke in me a shuddering sixth sense, vaguely compounded of fear, ecstatic happiness and a wild inexplicable sentiment that resembled nothing so nearly as a consciousness of guilt.

"Judge then, with what wondering, unbelievable joy, I received in your well known MS. the Valentine which first gave me to see that you know me to exist.

"The idea of what men call Fate lost then in my eyes its character of futility. I felt that nothing hereafter was to be doubted, and lost myself for many weeks in one continuous, delicious dream, where all was a vivid, yet indistinct bliss.

"Immediately after reading the Valentine, I wished to contrive some mode of acknowledging—without wounding you by seeming directly to acknowledge—my sense— oh, my keen—my exulting—my ecstatic sense of the honor you had conferred upon me. To accomplish as I wished it, precisely *what* I wished, seemed impossible, however;

and I was on the point of abandoning the idea, when my
eyes fell upon a volume of my own poems; and then the
lines I had written, in my passionate boyhood, to the first
purely ideal love of my soul—to the Helen Stanard of
whom I told you—flashed upon my recollection. I
turned to them. They expressed all—*all* that I would
have said to you—so fully—so accurately and so exclusively, that a thrill of intense superstition ran at once
through my frame. Read the verses and then take into
consideration the peculiar need I had at the moment, for
just so seemingly an unattainable mode of communication with you as they afforded. Think of the absolute
appositeness with which they fulfilled that need—expressing not only all that I would have said of your person,
but all that of which I most wished to assure you, in the
lines commencing,

On desperate seas long wont to roam

Think of the rare agreement of name, and you will
no longer wonder that to one accustomed as I am to the
Calculus of Probabilities, they wore an air of absolute
miracle—I yielded at once to an overwhelming sense of
Fatality. From that hour I have never been able to
shake from my soul the belief that my Destiny, for good
or for evil, either here or hereafter, is in some measure
interwoven with your own.

"Of course I did not expect, on your part, any acknowledgment of the printed lines 'To Helen'; and yet,
without confessing it to myself, I experienced an indefinable sense of sorrow in your silence. At length, when
I thought that you had had time fully to forget me (if,
indeed, you had ever really remembered) I sent you the

anonymous lines in MS. I wrote, first, through a pin-
ing, burning desire to communicate with you in *some*
way—even if you remained in ignorance of your correspondent. The mere thought that *your* dear fingers
would press—*your* sweet eyes dwell upon the characters
which *I* had penned—characters which had welled out
upon the paper from the depths of so devout a love—
filled my soul with a rapture, which seemed, then, all
sufficient for my human nature. It *then* appeared to
me that merely one thought involved so much of bliss
that here on earth I could have no right to repine—no
room for discontent. If ever, *then,* I dared to picture for myself a richer happiness, it was always connected with your image in Heaven. But there was yet
another idea which impelled me to send these lines:—I
said to myself the sentiment—the holy passion which
glows in my bosom *for her,* is of Heaven, heavenly, and
has no taint of the earth. Thus then must lie in the
recesses of her own pure bosom, at least the germ of a
reciprocal love, and if this be indeed so, she will need
no earthly clue—she will instinctively feel who is her
correspondent— In this case, then, I may hope for
some faint token at least, giving me to understand that
the source of the poem is known and its sentiments comprehended even if disapproved.

"O God!—how long—*how long* I have waited in *vain*
—hoping against hope—until, at length, I became possessed with a spirit far sterner—far more reckless than
despair—I explained to you—but without detailing the
vital influences they wrought upon my fortune—the
singular additional, yet seemingly trivial fatality by
which you happened to address your anonymous stanzas

to Fordham instead of New York—by which my aunt
happened to get notice of their being in the West Farm
post-office. But I have not yet told you that your lines
reached me in Richmond on the very day in which I was
about to enter on a course which would have borne me far,
far away from *you*, sweet, sweet Helen, and from this
divine dream of your love."

Poe, it is obvious from this letter, had lost his grip
upon the fancies which had always haunted him and lost,
too, the power to give them imaginative form. What
we have here is the raw material of his art, madness un-
transmuted by genius. He no longer had the power
which he had once had of subliming his vague irrational
emotions into poetry, for when he sought to express in
verse the same feelings which had once stirred him he
was compelled to abandon the attempt and to fall back
upon what he had once written long long ago; and yet
these emotions mastered him more completely than they
ever had before.

The silly woman whom he addressed was far from being a satisfactory embodiment of that dream Helen
whose shadowy form had led him home to his world of
strange beauty but she was the best that was available
and so far had he lost touch with reality that he could
fancy that he saw in her tawdry eccentricities the unearthly charm of the figure that haunted him. For the
moment at least even Virginia was forgotten since, so
this letter states, even in Heaven it was to be not with her
but with this new Helen that he was to be united, and
yet somewhere in his mind was a realization of the difficulty which faced him. He could guess that Mrs. Whitman, was, physically, a normal woman, that marriage

with her would entail the physical union of which he was for some reason incapable, and so it was that as he felt himself drawn to her there awoke in him "a shuddering sixth sense, vaguely compounded of fear, ecstatic happiness and a wild inexplicable sentiment that resembled nothing so nearly as a consciousness of guilt." In his subconsciousness he was warned, but he could not heed that warning.

Poe's conduct in the whole affair was that of a man who had a frenzied realization of the dilemma within which he was caught. In a whole series of letters, quite as extravagant as the one just quoted, he pressed his suit, declaring in one "Helen, I love now—for the first and only time," but no sooner had he won the lady's consent than his despair drove him into fits of intemperance which, as he must have foreseen, put an end to the preparations, already far advanced, for the marriage. It has been stated and it has been indignantly denied that almost upon the eve of the wedding he appeared before Mrs. Whitman in a state of complete intoxication and that he did this deliberately for the purpose of escaping from a marriage which he no longer desired, but whether or not Poe was conscious of his purpose is of little importance, for the fact remains that at the last moment he knew consciously or unconsciously that the wedding must never be and he either deliberately planned a rupture or in his despair was driven to excesses which accomplished his unrecognized purpose. How fully aware he was of the cause of his distress we shall never know, but it was when brought face to face with the prospect of a real marriage that he lost the last shreds of his sanity. Certain it is that after he had first received a conditional promise from Mrs. Whitman the effect was so far from joyous that he returned to Fordham so changed, according to Mrs. Clemm, that she hardly recognized him; and certain also that at the same time (November 1848) he wrote to another of his women friends ("Annie") a letter which spoke of his future plans without any reference to Mrs. Whitman and which called the recipient of this letter "My own sweet *sister* Annie, my pure beautiful angel."

During this period Poe was flinging himself at any woman who crossed his path. The whole of the female sex seemed merged into one and he hardly distinguished between them, calling out as he did to one and all to "save" him from he knew not what. One of the letters to this same Annie will illustrate his abysmal weakness.

"How," he writes, "shall I explain to you the *bitter, bitter* anguish which has tortured me since I left you? You saw, you *felt* the agony of grief with which I bade you farewell—you remember my expression of gloom—of a dreadful, horrible foreboding of Ill. Indeed—*indeed* it seems to me that Death approached me even then, and that I was involved in the shadow which went before him. . . . I said to myself—'it is for the last time, until we meet in Heaven.' I remember nothing distinctly from that moment until I found myself in Providence. I went to bed and wept through a long, long, hideous night of Despair—when the day broke, I arose and endeavored to quiet my mind by a rapid walk in the cold, keen air—but all *would* not do—the Demon tormented me still. Finally, I procured two ounces of laudanum, and, without returning to my hotel took the cars back to Boston. When I arrived I wrote you a letter, in which I opened

my whole heart to you—to *you*. . . . I told you how
my struggles were more than I could bear. . . . I then
reminded you of that holy promise which was the last
I exacted from you in parting—the promise that, under
all circumstances, you would come to me on my bed of
death. I implored you to come *then*, mentioning the
place where I should be found in Boston. Having written this letter, I swallowed about half the laudanum and
hurried to the Post Office,—intending not to take the
rest until I saw you—for, I did not doubt for one moment, that Annie would keep her sacred promise. But
I had not calculated on the strength of the laudanum,
for, before I reached the Post Office my reason was entirely gone, and the letter never put in. Let me pass
over—my darling *sister*—the awful horrors which succeeded. A friend was at hand, who aided and (if it
can be called saving) saved me, but it was only within
the last three days that I have been able to remember
what occurred in that dreary interval. It appears that,
after the laudanum was rejected from the stomach, I became calm, and—to a casual observer, sane—so that I
was suffered to go back to Providence . . . It is not *much*
that I ask, *sweet sister Annie*—my mother and myself
would take a small cottage at—oh, *so* small—so *very*
humble—I should be far away from the tumult of the
world—from the ambition which I loathe—I would labor
day and night, and with industry, I could accomplish *so*
much. Annie! It would be a Paradise beyond my wildest hopes—I could see some of your beloved family *every*
day, and you often . . . Do not these pictures touch your
inmost heart? . . . I am at home now with my dear
mother who is endeavoring to comfort me—but the sole

words which soothe me are those in which she speaks of Annie—she tells me that she has written you, begging you to come to Fordham. Ah, Annie, *is it not possible?* I am so *ill*—so terribly, hopelessly *ill* in body and mind, that I CANNOT live, unless I can feel your sweet, gentle loving hand pressed upon my forehead—oh, my *pure, virtuous, generous, beautiful sister* Annie! Is it not POSSIBLE for you to come—if only for one little week? Until I subdue this fearful agitation, which, if continued, will either destroy my life or drive me hopelessly mad. Farewell—*here and hereafter—forever your own,* Eddy."

A little later he was writing to the same lady *à propos* Mrs. Whitman: "But of one thing rest assured, 'Annie'—from this day forth I shun the pestilential society of *literary women.* They are a heartless, unnatural venemous, dishonorable *set,* with no guiding principles but inordinate self-esteem. Mrs. Osgood is the *only* exception I know."

Meanwhile, Poe was exhibiting various other signs of mental disintegration. During the two and a half years of life which remained to him after the death of Virginia his mind was feverishly at work with the extravagant and feebly pretentious speculations which were to be embodied in *Eureka.* Almost immediately after the death of his wife he began to meditate upon the riddle of existence and, relying upon scraps of scientific knowledge (much of it grossly inaccurate), he attributed an absurd value to his speculations. By February 1848 he was ready to give a lecture on *The Cosmography of the Universe,* but instead of the hundreds of people whom he expected to hear him, some sixty turned up at the Society

Library and listened to a rhapsody of which the reporters for the newspapers, at least, could make neither head nor tail. Poe, however, felt his confidence by no means shaken. Sitting down to write, he began:

"It is with humility really unassumed—it is with a sentiment even of awe—that I pen the opening sentence of this work; for of all conceivable subjects I approach the reader with the most solemn—the most comprehensive—the most difficult—the most august.

"What terms shall I find sufficiently simple in their sublimity—sufficiently sublime in their simplicity—for the mere enunciation of my theme?

"I design to speak of the *Physical, Metaphysical and Mathematical—of the Material and Spiritual Universe—of its Essence, its Origin, its Creation, its Present Condition and its Destiny.* I shall be so rash moreover, as to challenge the conclusions, and thus, in effect, to question the sagacity, of many of the greatest and most justly reverenced men."

To this he added a preface in which he said *"What I here propound is true:*—therefore it cannot die:—if by any means it be now trodden down so as to die, it will 'rise again to the Life Ever Lasting' "—and then, completely in the grip of a delusion he hurried off to the offices of Wiley and Putnam.

As science, the intrinsic worth of the work in question is absolutely nil. The erroneous character of many of the alleged scientific facts upon which it was based has already been mentioned in a previous chapter, and it may be added that far from having any conception of fact as fact Poe made no general effort to familiarize himself with the works of genuine scientists, and, though he had read Humboldt's *Cosmos*, when a friend wrote to him concerning one of the most important works of his generation (*Vestiges of Creation*) he scorned to read it and only asked his friend to tell him how far the ideas of *Vestiges* were coincident with such propositions of his own as the following: "Unity is nothingness" and "All matter springing from unity sprang from nothingness." Yet though Poe's speculations, so confused and so self-contradictory as to be well nigh incomprehensible, are not worth discussion for their own sake, there is much in the tenor of them which throws light upon his insanity and which shows it to be intimately connected with the more controlled aberrations which gave birth to his art. *Eureka* is simply the product of a mind which has been completely mastered by the fancies which it had once been able to control and use.

The death of Virginia removed, as has been said, the keystone from the elaborate structure of rationalizations which constituted his mental life. When she was gone the whole legend by which he lived inevitably collapsed and he was suddenly faced with the necessity of building it anew. Whereas in the former days he had been able to satisfy his neurotic need for a sense of greatness by the exercise of his genuine powers and by an artistically handled pretense to a learning and philosophical profundity which he did not have, he was now, in his greater need, driven to a process of more gigantic self-deception. No humanly possible achievement was great enough for him and he must become the greatest man of all time, he must solve the riddle of the universe, track God to His lair and identify himself with the soul of the Cosmos. "My whole nature utterly *revolts*" he exclaimed, "at the idea there is any being in the Universe superior to *myself*" and in that utterance is the key to *Eureka* which is, psychologically, merely a delusion of grandeur.

Mr. Putman himself was in the office when Poe arrived with the manuscript. Poe entered in a somewhat nervous and excited manner, declaring that he wished to discuss a matter of the highest importance. "Seated at my desk, and looking at me a full minute with his glittering eye," writes Putnam, "he at length said: 'I am Mr. Poe.' I was all ear, of course, and sincerely interested in the author of 'The Raven' and 'The Gold Bug.' 'I hardly know,' said the poet, after a pause, 'how to begin with what I have to say. It is a matter of profound importance.' After another pause, the poet, seeming to be in a tremor of excitement, went on to say that the publication he had to propose was of momentous interest. Newton's discovery of gravitation was a mere incident compared with the discoveries revealed in this book. It would at once command such universal and intense interest that the publisher might give up all other enterprises and make this book the business of his lifetime. An edition of fifty thousand might be sufficient to begin with; but it would be a small beginning. No other scientific event in the history of the world would approach in importance the original developments of this book. All this and more, not in irony or in jest, in *intense* earnestness—for he held me with his eye like the Ancient Mariner. I was really impressed, but not overcome. Promising a decision on Monday (it was late Saturday P. M.), the poet had to rest so long in uncertainty upon the *extent* of the edition—partly reconciled by a small loan, meanwhile. We *did* venture, not upon fifty thousand, but five hundred. Even after this edition was in type the poet proposed to punish us by giving a duplicate of the MS to another publisher because a third little cdvance was deemed inexpedient."

All his life Poe had been the victim of such delusions but they had been to a certain extent under control. They had spurred him on to achievement and he had embodied them in gorgeous dreams, but now the line between the fantasy and actuality, always a little uncertain, had completely disappeared and he believed completely in things which had formerly been only half real. He had, as it were, kept himself sane by the projection, in the form of fiction, of the self he liked to imagine himself to be, but he could no longer maintain the distinction. Now he felt himself actually the master of the secrets which Roderick Usher strove to penetrate, and instead of making his claim to them indirectly and half fancifully through the portraiture of imaginary people he came forward to demand that the public recognize in him the dream of greatness which had haunted him. No longer capable of the slightest self-criticism, he huddled together all the scraps of science and metaphysics which he could remember. The materialist's theory of the atoms he mingled with transcendental ideas, borrowed probably from Coleridge, concerning the individual's intuitive knowledge of God; to this he added a pantheistic conception of an all-pervasive deity, part of whom is resident in every object, and then attempted to support the whole by vague references to Gravity, "which is but the

SARAH HELEN WHITMAN

From a portrait painted by John N. Arnold

mode in which is manifest the tendency of all things to return to their original unity," to the nebular hypothesis, and to the laws of Kepler concerning which he knew practically nothing whatever. So great was his need that it completely overcame his sanity and he really believed that, as he told Putnam, a publisher might regard the printing of his book as a complete business in itself.

It is, finally, worth noticing that this breakdown of Poe's sanity succeeded immediately upon his abandonment of his ostensible allegiance to reason. Because, as has been previously indicated, he recognized the danger to himself of the thoughts and fancies which came from he knew not where he had always exaggerated to himself the part which logic played in his mental processes and he had accepted nothing which he could not at least rationalize, but at the very beginning of *Eureka* he surrenders to the thing to which he had never before surrendered —a belief in mere intuition. All his life he had despised the transcendentalists, all his life he had clung to the belief that there was an ascertainable reason and logic behind everything, and as long as his mind demanded even that parody of reason called rationalization he could not accept the grandiose delusion embodied in *Eureka*. Now he wrote: "In the beginning, let me as distinctly as possible announce—not the theorem which I hope to demonstrate—for, whatever the mathematicians may assert, there is, in this world at least, *no such thing* as demonstration—but the ruling idea which, throughout this volume, I shall be continually endeavoring to suggest." He attempted to defend somehow this betrayal of his guiding principle by writing to a friend that "Intuition, after all, is but the conviction arising from those *inductions* or *de-*

ductions of which the processes are so shadowy as to escape our consciousness, elude our reason, or defy our capacity of expression," but what he had actually done was to cast off from the one mooring to which he had been held. There were brief moments when he half realized that *Eureka* was only a wild fancy but to have tolerated such a thought would have been to rob it of its whole *raison d'être* and so he was compelled in his own mind to equate imagination and truth.

"To the few who love me and whom I love—to those who feel rather than those who think—to the dreamers and those who put faith in dreams as the only realities— I offer this Book of Truths, not in its character of Truth-Teller, but for the Beauty that abounds in its truth; constituting it true. To these I present the composition as an Art-Product alone:—let us say a Romance; or, if I be not urging too lofty a claim, a Poem . . . What I here propound is true . . . Nevertheless it is as a poem only that I wish this work to be judged after I am dead."

The neurotic adjustment, however elaborate and ingenious it may be, is at best only a makeshift. Its victim is engaged in a battle against reality which he conducts by running away, but in the end reality always wins by demanding the complete surrender of the mind as the price of escape. The delusions may occupy, at first, but one corner of the mind; they may be hidden from the world or they may appear as mere eccentricities; but they are never wholly adequate. They must be continually enlarged to meet the new contingencies which constantly arise in the course of life and like a habit-forming drug they come finally to dominate the mind they served.

So it was with Poe. The compensation for his wounded

sense of pride, sprung from the humiliations of his childhood and aggravated by his psychic impotence, appeared
first as only an exaggerated ambition. His marriage
with the child Virginia served to hide the more dangerous
of his mental diseases, and by projecting his delusions in
the form of art he managed for many years to keep a precarious hold upon his sanity. But the death of his wife
brought him in contact with reality at the very point
where he could least bear such contact, with the result
that his delusions leaped almost immediately to an absolutely unmanageable magnitude. A fever of frustrated
eroticism seized upon him, his ambition developed quickly
into a genuine delusion of grandeur, his intemperance
grew more and more appalling, and he fell victim to
various subsidiary delusions.

By July 1848 he had become completely incapable
of taking care of himself. In a fantastic hope of being
able to raise money to found a magazine of his own, he
had gone at that time to Richmond but when he arrived
there he entered upon a fortnight's debauch in one of
the lowest haunts upon the wharves of the city from
which he was rescued by John R. Thompson, then editor
of the *Messenger*, who reports: "I did all I could to re-
strain his excesses and to relieve the pressure of his immediate wants (he was extremely indigent) but no influence was adequate to keep him from the damnable
propensity to drink, and his entire residence in Richmond
of late was but a succession of disgraceful follies."
Already he was speaking of himself to Thompson as "the
victim of a preordained damnation, as *l'ame perdue*, a
soul lost beyond all hope of redemption," and when he
returned to New York to make the final breach with

Mrs. Whitman it was probably with a sense that for him all was over. His irrational melancholy was settling more and more deeply upon him: "My sadness," he writes to "Annie," "is *unaccountable* and this makes me the more sad. I am full of dark forebodings. *Nothing* cheers or comforts me. My life seems wasted—the future looks a dreary blank; but I will struggle on and 'hope against hope.'" And when on June 30, 1849 he had finished his preparations for the last fatal journey to Richmond he called upon Mrs. Lewis, one of the women who had befriended him, to tell her, "I have a presentiment that I shall never see you again. I must leave to-day for Richmond. If I never return, write my life. You can and will do me justice."

When he arrived at Philadelphia, the first stage of his journey, he fell victim to an attack of insanity which took the form of a delusion of persecution. Calling upon John Sartain, whom he had known during his residence in Philadelphia, he demanded from him protection against assassins. "He said that it would be difficult for me to believe what he had to tell, or that such things were possible in this nineteenth century . . . He told me that he had been on his way to New York, but he had heard some men who sat a few seats back of him plotting how they should kill him and then throw him off the platform of the car. He said they spoke so low that it would have been impossible for him to hear and understand the meaning of their words, had it not been that his sense of hearing was so wonderfully acute . . . From this fear of assassination his mind gradually veered around to an idea of self-destruction, and his words clearly indicated this tendency . . . After a long silence he said suddenly,

188

'If this mustache of mine was removed I should not be so easily recognized; will you lend me a razor, that I may shave it off?'

"He said that he had been thrown in Moyamensing Prison for forging a check and while there a white female figure had appeared on the battlements and had addressed him in whispers. 'If I had not heard what she said,' he declared, 'it would have been the end of me.'

" 'An attendant asked me if I would like to take a stroll about the place. I might see something interesting and I agreed. In the course of our rounds on the ramparts we saw a cauldron of burning spirits. He asked me if I would not like to take a drink. I declined, but, had I said yes, I should have been lifted over the brim and dipped into the hot liquid, up to the lips like Tantalus. . . . So at last as a means to torture me and to wring my heart, they brought out my mother, Mrs. Clemm, to blast my sight by seeing them first saw off her feet to the ankles, then her legs to the knees, her thighs at the hips!' "

On the second morning after his arrival at Sartain's home he was, however, sufficiently recovered to recognize that the story which he had told was the result of a delusion but though he soon seemed well enough to continue his journey he was enjoying only a temporary sanity. In a letter written to Mrs. Clemm and sent, apparently, from Philadelphia he said:

"I have been ill—have had the cholera, or spasms quite as bad, and can now hardly hold the pen.

"The very instant you get this come to me. The joy of seeing you will almost compensate for our sorrows. We can but die together. It is no use to reason with

189

me now; I must die. I have no desire to live since I have done *Eureka*. I could accomplish nothing more. For your sake it would be sweet to live, but we must die together. You have been all in all to me, darling, ever beloved mother, and dearest, truest friend.

"I was never really insane, except on occasions where my heart was touched.

"I have been taken to prison once since I came here for getting drunk; but then I was not. It was about Virginia."

It is evident that Poe betook himself to Richmond with a heart which had already surrendered and which clung to nothing except his final grandiose delusion—the importance of *Eureka*. A week later he was writing from that city another impassioned appeal to Mrs. Clemm: "I got here with two dollars over—of which I enclose you one. O God, my mother, shall we ever meet again? If possible, oh COME! My clothes are so horrible and I am so ill. Oh, if you could come to me, my mother. Write instantly— Oh do not fail. God forever bless you."

Yet in spite of this he managed once more to get some sort of hold upon himself, to find friends to aid him, to deliver a lecture and even to get himself again engaged, this time to the widow Mrs. Shelton who had been in youth his first sweetheart—Miss Royster. A little later, however, he fell once more into his old courses. Frantic letters from Mrs. Clemm show that she had lost knowledge of him, and (the fact is perhaps not insignificant) it was upon a return trip to New York for the purpose of completing arrangements for his marriage

to Mrs. Shelton that he came to his death in the mysterious manner recounted in the first chapter of this study.

Doubtless we shall never know the details of the event
and they are after all of minor importance.   Death alone
could free him from the web of desires and delusions
which his disease had spun and death in one form or
another was imminent.   During a period of two and a
half years he had clearly demonstrated the fact that with
Virginia gone he could not possibly reconstruct another
life illusion by which he could live, and life, which had
doubtless never been for him worth living, now became
intolerable.   It was a burden to him and to others; his
mental disorder was no longer productive of his weirdly
beautiful visions, and even had he lived to write he would
probably have written only obscurer and more frenzied
Eurekas.   Death robbed posterity of nothing worth the
having, it set both him and his friends free from a long
endured misery, and it was welcome even though it had
to come as it did in a shape so sordid and so mean.

VIII

THE works of Poe have no place in the American literary tradition, for though their defects are sometimes those of a time or a place, their virtues are isolated and self-contained. The sentimental melodrama of some of his inferior pieces and the not infrequent provinciality of his literary judgments are often traceable to his environment, but both the materials with which he worked and the genius which transformed them came wholly from within. That his life happened to fall between the years 1809 and 1849 is merely an accident, and he has no more in common with Whittier, Lowell, Longfellow, or Emerson than he has with either the eighteenth or nineteenth centuries in England.

In any society Poe would have been an outcast. He might have had the good fortune to be born, like Baudelaire, in a world a little more tolerant of outcasts than that of literary America in the early nineteenth century; in an older and richer civilization he might have found habitable circles outside respectability where he would not have been compelled constantly to measure himself by the standards of a bourgeois society; he might, in a word, have finally adapted himself to a Bohemia had one existed; but under any imaginable circumstance he would have been outcast and miserable.

His works bear no conceivable relation, either external or internal, to the life of any people, and it is impossible to account for them on the basis of any social or intellectual tendencies or as the expression of the spirit of any age. There are, of course, those with whom he is spiritually kin, but they belong to no particular nation or time. Wherever and whenever the members of his race are born they are always alien to their fellows and they are related to one another by virtue of the very things which cut them off from the majority. In America he had no ancestors and no real descendants.

Paul Elmer More is the only critic who has ever attempted to account for him historically. Poe's diabolism, says More, is merely the second attenuation of the Puritan preoccupation with spiritual horror which becomes in Hawthorne an artistic attitude and, still further degenerated, appears in Poe as love for mere picturesque diablerie. But ingenious as this theory is and well as it might serve to explain some hypothetical writer, it does not fit the Poe we know. There is, in the first place, not the slightest indication that Poe, born of strolling players and educated as a Virginia gentleman, ever came in contact with even the most attenuated aspects of puritanism and, in the second place, no possibility of believing that his tales and poems were to him merely gruesome extravaganzas. One who had done no more than glance casually at a few of his pieces and who knew nothing of his life and personality might be excused for mistaking them (as both More and W. C. Brownell do) for mere artifice, but in the light of the intimate relationship which exists between their tone and the tone of his life there can be no question but that they are genuine and sincere expressions of a real mind. He can in a measure be explained; he has his literary affinities;

but the explanation is rather psychological than historical and both his genesis and his significance are to be
found by reference not to any tradition or environment
but instead to the morbid type to which he belongs.

It is this fact which accounts more than any other for
the extraordinary divergence in the critical estimates
which have been made of Poe. John Burroughs, writing in the *Dial* for October 16, 1893, undertakes to explain to Edmund Gosse why no work of Poe's appeared in the list of the ten best American books com-
piled shortly before by the readers of a New York
literary journal. "It is probably true," says Burroughs, "that the world of readers generally cares less
and less for poets of the Poe, the Swinburne, the Rossetti
type. . . . Poe's literary genius, as such, was undoubtedly of a high order, higher in some respects than that of
Whittier or Longfellow or Lowell; but he was much less
than these men in other important respects. . . . Back of
his literary and artistic talent what is there? Not a
large, brotherly, helpful man . . . With the coming of
science, of democracy, of the industrial age, there has
come in a new spirit, which demands of the book or the
poem, 'What is it for? What message has it for struggling, thinking men?' "

Now Burroughs was here expressing the common
protest of the plain man against all non-didactic
art. Poe had been often enough rebuked in much the
same terms before, and such an attitude is alone sufficient
to explain why critics of a certain type should not think
very highly of him. The most significant voice of dissent does not, however, come from men of this sort.
That they should fail to appreciate him may be taken as

a matter of course but there is an equally great divergence among those whose varying estimates must be explained in a different way. Edmund Gosse considers Poe as, on the whole, the greatest literary genius which America has produced, while Henry James regarded a liking for Poe's poetry as a sure sign of undeveloped taste. The divergence is not due to any insistence on James's part upon the utilitarian function of art, but rather to a blindness which he has in common with a large number of people who are by temperament incapable of either perceiving or appreciating an essentially morbid beauty.

It is not only those who judge literature by its moral effect but also those who judge it by the amount of intelligence which it reveals who are bound to put a low estimate upon Poe's work. Young people and sentimentalists sometimes exhibit a considerable liking for the merely external melodrama in which he abounds, but to mature critics like More and Brownell it is bound to seem mere artifice unless they happen to have chords in their temperaments which respond to the neurotic melodies which are the secret of his fascinations. A really kindred spirit like Baudelaire is raised to a pitch of admiration which seems positively insane to those who are, happily perhaps, without even a touch of the morbidity to which he appeals and, in general, the critical estimate of Poe varies directly with the critic's sensitivity to the minor melodies perceptible to some even amidst the most obvious melodramatics of *The Raven*.

Any true estimate of the value of Poe's imaginative work must, then, begin with a recognition of his limitations, and they are, perhaps, narrower than those of any other writer who has aroused a comparable amount of

admiration. The ambiguity of his position in the literature of the world has only been increased by the uncriti-
cal claims of his American cult, for that cult has been
largely composed not of those who have had any temperamental affinity with him but rather of those who
have taken a childish delight in his ingenious melodrama
and have been patriotically eager to advance him as an
American claimant to international literary honors. Not
only have they sentimentalized his legend but they have
at the same time postponed any general recognition of
his right to the domain which is really his by their failure
to define its limits. They have wished, for example, to
include among his achievements the poetic expression of
normal sentiment, and to that end they have empha-
sized some of the mere conventional exercises in verse
which are little better or worse than similar efforts by
the female poets he so much admired; they have pretended that he would have liked to claim credit for the
mechanical formula of the contemporary short story;
they have even attempted to find some basis for admiring
the profundity of *Eureka;* and they have, at the same
time, done all they could to explain away the secret of
his genuine power. The typical American admirer of
Poe has been, in a word, a person anxious to have him
admired for any reasons except the legitimate one.

Leaving aside for the present any consideration of
his critical work, of its relation to his own temperament,
of its influence, and of its absolute value, it is evident
that his imaginative writings have an authenticity in
direct proportion to the intimacy of their connection
with the abnormal states of his mind. He rarely attempted and never succeeded in picturing anything vis-

ible to the people for whom he wrote. There are, it is true, traces here and there of bits of landscape which he had observed in his lonely walks, but it is very near the absolute truth to say that for him the American scene was non-existent. He gave no picture of the life of his times, and it would be hard to find any other writer whose works are so completely valueless as documents for the study of the thought of an age. In so far as they tell us of anything besides himself they tell us of those neurotic kinsmen of his whose kinship, purely psychological, has nothing to do with either the race to which they belong, the land in which they were born, or the time in which they lived.

In spite of those who advised him to do so, Poe wrote no novels and he wrote no stories of the sort which could come home to the hearts and bosoms of his readers because he was absolutely incapable of being interested in any of the things in which they were normally interested. When he undertook to write a long piece he drew his material from a book of travels because the scenes there described were sufficiently remote to be absorbed directly into his mind, but so completely was his vision turned inward upon himself that he was incapable of observation in the ordinary sense. Nor was he to any less absolute degree devoid of what is called an understanding of human character. In life the motives which he attributed to the people with whom he came in contact were always fantastic. The Longfellow, the Lowell, the Mrs. Whitman and the Virginia whom he imagined were, like such abstractions as the Bostonian, not real people but figments of a distorted imagination, and in his work he created no real characters for his people were invariably merely projections of himself. It cannot be said that he had any knowledge or experience of what is called life or that in his forty years of existence he learned anything of anybody except himself. The only psychology with which his work shows any familiarity is abnormal psychology and the only springs of action concerning which he reveals knowledge are the morbid ones by which he himself was influenced. Motives are completely absent from his people; it is only obsessions that he can analyze.

Even those few prejudices which served him in lieu of an attitude toward the outside world are visible only here and there in his writings. By his contemporaries he was credited with a variety of sinister opinions. His social ideas were spoken of as cynically individualistic, his religious attitude as atheistic, and his moral code as a mere nihilism. But so completely negative were these opinions that they rarely appear in his writings. He did it is true express a distrust of the whole democratic idea in one of his reviews, and he did give it clearly to be understood by *Eureka* that his theism approached close to a mere materialistic conception of a universal force, but he rarely says anything explicit capable of shocking the most orthodox. Unlike most of those who dissent from currently accepted notions he had no real interest in this dissent and, except in the realm of literary judgment, had in him nothing of the spirit of the iconoclast. Though it was known (says Mrs. Weiss) to his intimate friends that his theism was in no sense Christian and though (according to Briggs) he thought the Bible a mere rigmarole, he would answer in response to a question that he was an Episcopalian (that having been the religion of the Allan household in which he had been brought up), and the at-

titude here exhibited is typical. He shocked people by
the ghastliness of his visions, but on the whole he tended
to conceal rather than to display those intellectual convic-
tions which were unorthodox. They were the results
rather than the causes of his general state of mind and he
had, as a writer, only an incidental concern with them.
To say as so many of his unfavorable critics have said
that his works inculcate no useful moral lesson is to hit
upon an absurdly small part of the negative aspect of his
writings, for they exist in a complete moral vacuum and
cannot possibly teach any lesson moral or immoral since
questions of morality never enter into them. Any moral
code, even the diabolistic, presupposes the existence of
at least two people, but to Poe no one except himself
was real enough to be interesting.

The lives of his characters touch the life of the world
at large at no single point. Doubtless because of Poe's
own frustrated longing for the privileges of the aristocrat he liked to imagine them as the descendants of
a noble line living in gloomy self-sufficiency, but even
when they are not specifically privileged by birth they
are invariably isolated and freed from the necessity of
those contacts which the possession of a family or the
duties of a profession entail. They earn no living, they
engage in no regular occupation, and they have no social
duties. The problems which they face and the catastro-
phes which they suffer are always such as concern them
alone, and so the whole circle of social problems is removed
along with everything that concerns morals or ethics
from his work. Even the crimes which his heroes commit
awaken no echoes outside themselves, and neither law nor
public opinion exists except when, as in the case of *The*

Murders in the Rue Morgue, their function is purely subsidiary; they form no part of the real subject-matter of
the tale. Poe is interested in the soul's relation to itself
but in nothing else.

Thus it is evident that nearly all the things which ordinarily give value to a piece of literature are absent
from Poe's work. The whole realm of moral ideas is excluded not merely as morality *per se* but also as artistic
material used for the creation of conflicts and situations;
no characters are created, no social problems presented,
and no normal psychology exemplified. Horror and
logic—logic exercising itself upon the most abstract and
remote of materials, horror which deliberately invents the
causes for itself—these are the only two subjects which
are genuinely his own, and they are in reality but one
subject since the logic is, functionally, only a temporary
surcease from horror. Even that horror, appearing
though it does in various guises, is of one kind only, for
it is always a pure emotion without any rational foundation. It is not based upon any fundamentally pessimis-
tic philosophy or upon any concern with the sorrows of
the world. Poe does not, like Artzibashef, for instance,
present any examples from, or allegories of, the common
lot of misery; to the still sad music of humanity he is con-
genitally tone-deaf; he speaks for himself and for himself alone.

There are, it is true, many in whom his voice sets hidden chords in vibration, many whose answering response
comes from secret, half unrecognized sources, who become
suddenly aware of faint memories of or dimly recognized
potentialities for the emotions to which he gives utterance; there are, also, some few like Mallarmé and Baude-

laire who seem to hear in his speech the utterance of their own souls, and who arise to proclaim him their spokesman. Yet of neither of these groups was Poe very distinctly aware. His cry, sometimes so harsh and sometimes so musical, comes from the depth of his own lonely soul. It rings over a world with whose problems he was as little concerned as it was, in general, with him, and it falls upon the ear like a voice from an abyss. Unearthly and distant, it seems almost unreal; but then, just as we have dismissed it as some trick or some illusion, it curdles the blood, for we have caught an accent that cannot be mistaken. The voice is unmistakably terrible.

His gift, then, is the gift of expression, but even as such the gift is limited in the things expressed almost exclusively to his own emotions and to the deductions which his elaborately rationalizing mind can make from them. To a neurotically deranged temperament is superadded, paradoxically, a power of clear arrangement which constitutes him a genius. Thanks to it he is able to unify his obsessions and delusions into a system which serve him as a philosophy and a *weltanschauung* by which he can live; thanks to it also he can give to his descriptions of his world an appearance of orderliness and self-consistence which make it temporarily real to his readers. From his early experiment in pseudo-realistic narration (*The Narrative of Arthur Gordon Pym*) it would appear that he learned a lesson from Defoe, for he certainly had there caught Defoe's secret of making terrible things creditable by the circumstantial recounting of realistic details, but he had already developed a technique of his own more suitable to the short tale in which he excelled. For the diffuse formlessness of Defoe he substitutes a mathematically, almost mechanically, neat form in which each incident and each word is arranged with a conscious art which no effort is made to conceal. Recognizing the unfamiliarity of his material he is willing, if necessary, to sacrifice everything to perfect clarity. Thus his expositions follow the form of logical demonstration; his incidents are often brutally simple and nakedly physical because there must be no possibility of misunderstanding them, but the intention cannot be mistaken.

We may imagine, perhaps, that his gift of exposition was cultivated by practice upon himself. If he was to maintain his sanity his fantasies must seem to him reasonable and accountable; he explains and justifies them to himself; and in so doing he learns how they may be made to seem most reasonable to others. Morbid psychology he takes for granted because it was the only psychology familiar to him; he speaks of the pleasure which "we" take in the contemplation of the incident in the Black Hole in Calcutta or any similar example of torture on a large scale; he assumes that the imp of the perverse which leads people to do things for no other reason except that they are wrong is as familiar to everybody as it is to him; and he takes it for granted that we are as accustomed as he is to the night terrors which seize him; but after starting with this assumption, his expositions are singularly complete and his descriptions realize entirely the effect which he has had in mind. Because he has no delicacy where horror is concerned, because he stops at nothing, he never falls short. Once he has started there is no relenting. He recoils in disgust from no physical horror and hesitates in the full analysis of no terrible depth of perversity.

When he fails it is usually because he has attempted
something outside his narrow range. Occasionally (especially in his verse) he does not succeed in differentia-
ting with sufficient sharpness between his own morbid
melancholy and ordinary sentimentality or melodrama,
but in his prose stories he almost invariably succeeds except when he is led away from the moods which are real
to him. He could not, for example, though he tried
often, be humorous, because he had not one trace of humor
in his make-up and fancied that it consisted in mere mechanical facetiousness. He would begin drearily enough,
and then in spite of himself he would veer round to the
subjects which alone interested him, and his comic tale
would degenerate into a jauntily delivered list of horrors.
In one a young man who is later hanged thus describes
his experiences: "I was here, accordingly, thrown out at
the sign of Crow (by which tavern the coach happened to
be passing) without meeting with any farther accident
than the breaking of both my arms under the left hind
wheel of the vehicle. I must besides do the driver justice
to state that he did not forget to throw after me the
largest of my trunks, which, unfortunately falling on my
head, fractured my skull in a manner at once interesting
and extraordinary."

In another a lady who has climbed a belfry for the sake
of the view puts her head through a hole in the clock face
only to find it caught there by one of the hands of the
clock, the climax of the comedy being the moment when
the decapitated head rolls down the roof and bounces from
the guttering to the street below. But though the amuse-
ment which Poe himself may have been able to derive from
such tales was not communicable it was the only one of his

emotions which he did not succeed in making real. To those who have in them only that faint trace of the morbidity which is so commonly an accompaniment of artistic sensitivity he opens the doors to the whole paradise of pleasurable pains amidst which the neurotic dwell. If "there is a pleasure in being mad that only madmen know" then he has at least succeeded more nearly than any other writer in revealing it to the sane. His art is essentially one which makes it possible to visualize the gloomy magnificence of which he dreamed without sharing the derangement which gave birth to the dreams, to luxuriate in the voluptuous melancholy which surrounded him without being completely its victim, and, to put it as bluntly as possible, to experience the pleasurable emotion of the sadist without of necessity being one in reality.

It is for this reason that such influence as Poe's creative writing has had in America has been almost exclusively an influence upon form rather than upon matter or tone. He has been called *ad nauseam* "the father of the short story," and yet there is not a single American writer of importance, with the possible exception of Fitz-James O'Brien, whose work could be called like his. The rationalizing side of his mind led him to discover various technical devices which have been imitated by others, but those who have used them have rarely been in any sense spiritual kinsmen. Poe was the first to discuss the short story as a separate art-form and thus doubtless encouraged its cultivation, but nine tenths of the voluminous literature of brief fiction is essentially different in that it does not aim at the abstract, poetic, emotional effect of his tales but at the analysis of character, at the presentation of psychologi-

cal or social problems, or at mere plot ingenuity, and is
thus essentially nearer to the modern novel than to that
species of prose poem which Poe cultivated. Even the
law which he laid down concerning the single effect has
been interpreted in a sense a good deal larger than he intended and has come to mean no more than the mere
unity which every work of art must possess. Certainly
he founded no school here and it would be difficult indeed to prove that the course of American literature would
have been essentially different if he had never lived;
for, though it is natural for literary historians to assume that so important a writer was responsible for the
short story, the influence has never been satisfactorily
traced.

Even Ambrose Bierce, who seems, at first glance, more
nearly related than any other writer to Poe, will be found
upon analysis to be different in an essential particular.
He too depended largely upon horror, but unlike Poe
he would often base that horror upon the exaggeration
of a normal emotion. In, for example, a typical story
(*The Horseman in the Sky*) a son is compelled, in the
line of his duty as a soldier, to kill his father, and the
situation is Poesque in its ghastliness, but it depends for
its effect upon a normal emotion—family affection—
whereas it is just the distinguishing trait of Poe's horror that it never involves ordinary human feeling.
Bierce doubtless owed something to the earlier writer;
but the source and hence the effect of his mood was not
in a similar mental derangement. His bitterness, unlike
Poe's, is the result of a sense of the world's cruelty and
is thus essentially social as Poe's is essentially individualistic.

If one turns one's eyes toward Europe it becomes immediately evident that Poe passed on to Conan Doyle the detective story and to Jules Verne the idea of the pseudo-scientific romance. But here again it must be said that neither of these writers used the hint which he gave them in a manner to suggest the flavor as distinguished from the mechanics of a Poe story. Sherlock Holmes is ludicrously like Dupin both in himself and in his relations with his two foils—his more simple-minded companion and the bungling police—but the stories in which he figures are without those overtones for the sake of which Poe conceived his tales. In the case of Jules Verne the differences are even more strikingly evident. In his stories the interest is centered in the idea of scientific advance and he is half-way to H. G. Wells. In Poe, science has nothing to do with enthusiasm for mechanical invention or positivistic philosophy. In his early sonnet *To Science* he borrowed an idea from Keats in order to revile the very thing which Verne celebrates, and to Poe science was merely a new sort of hocus-pocus to be employed as he employed the names of mediæval books to suggest deeper mysteries. Conan Doyle and Jules Verne are daylight writers as essentially as Poe, even when he is most desperately rationalizing, is a writer whose scenes and moods belong at best to twilight regions.

He himself borrowed little of what is fundamentally important in him for the reason that he was the real inventor of the neurotic genre to which his work belonged and because of the peculiarity of his temperament he could pass his mood on only to those who were already prepared for it. Just as his own indebtedness to

"Gothic" and Germanic extravaganza was so slight that his works alone, among all those to which they might seem to be related, survive, so too most of those who are said to have been influenced by him have rather created new styles upon hints which he furnished than actually cultivated the region which was peculiarly his. His only real descendants are the so-called decadents—those that is to say who write with their nerves—and it is especially in France that they are to be found.

In the America of his day there was no one to whom he was not in some degree baffling, but it happened that his works had, all unknown to himself, sought out in France a spirit almost perfectly attuned to his own. In either 1846 or 1847 Charles Baudelaire, then a young man struggling to find means of expression, came by accident upon some fragments of Poe and, to use his own words, "saw with terror and delight not only the subjects I had dreamed of but *sentences* that I had thought of, and that he had written twenty years before." Almost immediately Baudelaire began his preparation for translating the major works of Poe, a task which occupied him for fifteen years, and to the very end he acknowledged with an ever-increasing enthusiasm that the American was the master who had taught him how morbidity might be made to blossom into *fleurs de mal*. Through Baudelaire the influence was passed on, and Poe, who had remained an isolated figure in his own country, became one of the chief forces which moulded that whole school of French writers which includes, among many of lesser rank, figures as great as Villiers de L'Isle Adam and Stéphane Mallarmé.

Thanks, perhaps, to the circumstances of his introduction and to the fact that he has there had followers whose works help to interpret him, France has never been, like America, at a loss in understanding the real provenance of Poe. Those who have felt themselves temperamentally unsympathetic have left him to those who would find no necessity to explain him away, and so though not all have praised him, none have failed to recognize his true nature. Though Saint-Beuve never could bring himself to compose the essay which Baudelaire urged him to write, and though Taine frankly confessed that he could not understand Poe's type of "the Germanic-Englishman with deep intuition and an amazingly overwrought nervous system," his position as the first of the great neurotics has never been questioned. To Baudelaire he is "l'ecrivain des nerfs"; to D'Aurevilly his work is "like a flower which has acquired strange new colorings and spotting because its roots have been dipped in poison"; and these opinions express in substance the judgment which a whole series of critics has passed upon him.

One of the earliest, Louis Étienne, wrote in 1857, "Oh for a breath of human feeling! That is what is lacking in these horrors which make you shudder." But the spokesmen for the schools whom Poe influenced find in him no lack. Morice in his "Littérature de toute à l'heure," one of the chief critical manifestoes of the Symbolists, included him with Chateaubriand, Goethe, Hugo, Balzac, Baudelaire, and Wagner as the producers of modern French literature, and adds; "He is the poet of Love in Fear, of Love in Madness, of Love in Death— the poet who in his divine works first inaugurated the poetic conscience—who painted the grotesque, not like

EUREKA:

A PROSE POEM.

BY

EDGAR A. POE.

NEW-YORK:
GEO. P. PUTNAM,
OF LATE FIRM OF "WILEY & PUTNAM,"
155 BROADWAY.
MDCCCXLVIII.

TITLE PAGE OF THE FIRST EDITION OF "EUREKA"

Victor Hugo to our eyes, but to our souls." To Péladan he is the "greatest genius of the nineteenth century,"
and Jules Lemaître in his "Dialogue des Morts" makes
him say: "You are right [in classing me with Plato and
Shakespeare]—I was indeed a sick man and a mad man;
I felt more than any one felt before me the terror of
the unknown, the dark, the mysterious, the inexplicable,
I was the poet of hallucination and of the dizziness of
the abyss; I was the poet of Fear. I developed in a
cold and exact style the secret logic of madness, and
experienced states of soul which the author of 'Hamlet'
himself barely guessed at twice or thrice. Perhaps it
might be right to say that I am less different from
Shakespeare than from Plato; but it is certain that we
are three specimens of the human race as different as
possible from each other."

From the very beginning America has fought against
this French view of Poe, and it is true that the judgment
of such critics as those just quoted is partially defective
as the result of a too exclusive admiration for the type
of literature which he represents. Poe "first inagurated
the poetic consciousness" only if there is no true poetry
except the poetry of morbid sensibility, and he is "the
greatest genius of the nineteenth century" only if the
works of such writers as Baudelaire and Mallarmé
are its most valuable productions. Moreover, distance
from the scene has made it possible for the French
writers to accept a romantic legend of Poe's life
and has led them to indulge in a good deal of rather
meaningless vituperation of the land that rejected
him.

Baudelaire believed that Poe's flight was less from him-

self than from the unsympathetic environment of
America. He worked himself into a frenzy of indigna-
tion against that "barbarie illuminé au gaz" which is
the United States and he added a picturesque phrase
to the literature of vituperation which Griswold has
inspired by remarking, "Il n'est donc pas en Amerique
d'ordenance qui interdise aux chiens l'entrée des cimi-
tières." Others followed him without stopping to remember that neither Belgium nor France accorded a
much better reception to his great translator, and thus
the legend of the persecuted genius has continued in
a slightly different form throughout Europe. Yet
whatever the defects of the French view may be as regards biography, and however exaggerated may be the
valuation which it has put upon Poe's peculiar quality,
it is difficult not to feel that the temperamental sympathy of the French has enabled them to describe and
analyze that quality more accurately than either
American or English critics.

In defiance of the plain evidence of the story of Poe's
life—the story of a man gradually disintegrating under
the influence of a nervous malady which finally conquers
him—and in defiance of the fact that his work contains
accurate description of various neurotic states concerning which it is difficult to believe that Poe could have
learned otherwise than by experience, it has been possible
for American critics to maintain that he was "the creator
of illusions, not the victim of illusions" and thus to stand
squarely in the way of any true understanding of his
work, while Baudelaire was enabled at the very beginning to guess the secret and to write: "The ardor with
which he throws himself into the grotesque for the love

of the grotesque and into the horrible for the love of the
horrible seems to me to prove the sincerity of his work and
the accord between the man and the poet. I have already remarked that, in the case of many men, this
ardor is often the result of a vast vital energy which
remains unoccupied, sometimes of a stubborn chastity
and of the suppression of a profound sensibility. The
unnatural pleasure which a man may feel in seeing his
own blood flow, sudden movements, violent and useless,
and cries hurled into the air when the spirit has not
given the command to the throat—these are phenomena
of the same order."

It is, indeed, only when he is viewed in this light that
it is possible to accord to Poe's creative writing any
significant position in the literature of the world. If
he is only a clever artificer who manipulated the stage
properties of melodrama, then he belongs in the limbo
where Ann Radcliffe reposes with Charles Brockden
Brown, and it would be merely an exhibition of American provinciality to claim for him any greater renown.
If his real descendants are Conan Doyle, Jules Verne,
and the innumerable professors of that mechanic art by
which popular fiction is written, then his position is
surely no higher than that of those whom he has taught
how to perform his tricks more successfully than he himself was ever able to do; while as for his verse, the best
criticism ever passed upon it must be contained in the
remarkable critique by N. P. Willis, who speaks of the
"exquisitely piquant and skillful exercise of rarity and
niceness of language" and "the curiosity in philologic
flavor" of *Ulalume*. Poe is then only "the jingle
man," as Emerson called him, and his "genius" contains

a good deal more than the "two fifths sheer fudge" estimated by Lowell.

An ingenious constructor both in prose and verse he certainly was. Not only did he become a master of rhyme and rhythm, of a mathematically exact construction, and a variety of stylistic tricks, but he not seldom utilized them to an illegitimate extent and thus fell into that artifice which, in the opinion of Baudelaire, gives to a work of art the additional charm of "rouge upon the cheeks of a beautiful woman." Yet it is not by these things that his worth is finally to be measured and he must stand or fall with the authors of that whole body of neurotic literature of which his works furnish the earliest complete example.

To evaluate an author, to affix as it were a price tag to his volumes, is never a task either very easy or very profitable and it becomes particularly useless in a case where, as with Poe, it is a question less of how well the thing was done than of the value of doing it. However many his failures, Poe, in the best of his stories and the best of his poems, succeeded supremely well and sometimes even in pieces heavily laden with dross there flash out lines of pure magic. The poet who was, even in the midst of a composition disfigured by vulgarisms, capable of lines like the following:

"Come! let the burial rite be read—the funeral song be sung!
An anthem for the queenliest dead that ever died so young—
A dirge for her the doubly dead in that she died so young

· · · · · · · · · ·

For her, the fair and debonair, that now so lowly lies,
The life upon her yellow hair but not within her eyes—
The life still there, upon her hair—the death upon her eyes"

was indisputably a master in his own particular way; and the prose writer who could compose *Berenice* and *The Tell-Tale Heart* has no superior in the creation of an atmosphere of morbid horror. Poe's preëminence is, moreover, recognized by those who continued in the school which he founded and upon such a matter they can best judge the extent of his originality. Poe is the real inventor of that *frisson nouveau* upon the discovery of which Hugo congratulated Baudelaire. One is bound to evaluate his works as one evaluates that discovery.

IX

THE PHILOSOPHY OF COMPOSITION

In "Modern Language Notes" for June, 1921, Professor Killis Campbell published the results of an extended investigation into the contemporary estimate of Poe. He shows conclusively that even after the success of *The Raven* the opinion of Poe's poetry in general was not sufficiently high to give him a place among the most important poets of the time, and also that it was rather as a critic than as a writer of fiction that his fame was greatest. "It does not," he adds, "affect the validity of this assertion to add that Poe was chiefly known as a fearless and caustic critic rather than a just and discriminating critic."

A considerable portion of this critical writing has inevitably lost some of its interest. Though its bulk is greater than that of any other species of composition which Poe undertook, much of it is concerned with the minute analysis of novels and poems which have long ceased, in any real sense, to exist. No living reader cares to have detailed to him through ten closely printed pages the plot of *Norman Leslie: A Tale of Present Times* or to have it pointed out that Mrs. L. H. Sigourney's poem *Zinzendorff* contains a passage "much injured by the occurrence of the word 'that' at the commencement of both the sixth and seventh line." Yet the fact that Poe was known "as a fearless and caustic critic" at a formative period in American literature when most

214

periodical criticism was as provincially tolerant as the Poet's Corner of a village newspaper is not without its significance. And still more important is the additional fact that scattered here and there through these casual reviews as well as systematically stated in more extended essays are critical opinions remarkable both for their unorthodoxy at the time when they were uttered and for their relation to a set of literary ideas just then in the process of growth. To-day Poe the critic is referred to quite as often as Poe the poet, or Poe the fictionist.

Though he gradually became very much interested in his theories, there is no reason to suppose that Poe had begun with any idea of becoming a critic or that he had any particular training for the exercise of that function. His formal education was early broken off, he had little time for extensive reading, and there is no evidence whatever that his familiarity with general literature was great. Just before he joined the staff of the *Messenger* he was in search of a livelihood, the position which was offered him promised that livelihood, and he undertook to review books as he undertook to discharge whatever other duties were expected of him. Thus he turned critic as many another young man has done, less because he had any particular desire to become one than because book-reviewing is a routine occupation for which no particular test of competence is required, and, like most others in his position, Poe did the best he could by displaying such knowledge as he happened to have whenever there was an opportunity and by hiding his ignorance as much as possible.

During the course of about a year he reviewed nearly a hundred books of very miscellaneous character, and while he devoted a good deal of space to rather trivial discussions of syntactical and other defects he developed rapidly his skill in the analysis of general propositions suggested by the work under discussion. He gave an enthusiastic reception to a translation of *I Promessi Sposi*, discussed Defoe in connection with a new edition of *Robinson Crusoe*, was surprisingly impressed by Longstreet's *Georgia Scenes*, and in a long review of Drake's poems drew the first and one of the most interesting of his elaborately maintained analyses, making here the distinction between the fancy displayed in *The Culprit Fay* and genuine imagination.

A supplement to the *Messenger* for July 1836 contains a reply by Poe to the various notices which the magazine had received and shows that in a very brief period what was regarded as a fearlessness bordering upon malicious severity had attracted widespread attention to his work. A remark in the course of the same article to the effect that the editor of a paper which had passed some strictures upon the *Messenger* is probably "the identical gentleman who once sent us from Newbern an unfortunate copy of verses" illustrates that tendency to petty and undignified bickering which Poe so abundantly indulged. The reputation which he had gained at this time was essentially of the sort which followed him to the other magazines in which his critical work appeared. From first to last, respect for him was somewhat discounted by that feeling of irritation which the *enfant terrible* always arouses.

In spite of his merits, it would be absurd to maintain that Poe's criticism did not show the effects of his lack of scholarship and his lack of general cultivation. Obscure names and quotations from foreign languages are scattered over his pages, but they are often, perhaps usually, borrowed from secondary sources; and though his reading, called extensive at the University of Virginia, was doubtless great for a college freshman, he suffered all his life from a sort of temporal provinciality as the result of the fact that both his knowledge and his tastes were largely confined to the works of his own half century and his own language. The English magazines he read extensively, and from them he borrowed much of his "learning," but he always gave the impression of knowing more than he did.

He rarely discusses any examples of the older literature, and when he does so it is generally with the assumption that his own generation has refined upon and improved the methods employed in former times. In this regard as in all others he could support his prejudices with ingenious reasoning, but it is usually impossible not to see in it the defense of an imperfectly cultivated taste.

"There is," he says, "about 'The Antigone,' as well as about all the ancient plays, an insufferable *baldness*, or platitude, the inevitable result of inexperience in Art— but a baldness nevertheless, which pedantry would force us to believe the result of a studied and supremely artistic simplicity alone. Simplicity is, indeed, a very lofty and very effective feature in all true art—but *not* the simplicity which we see in the Greek drama. . . . He [the Greek dramatist] did what he could—but that was exceedingly little worth. The profound sense of one or two tragic, or rather melo-dramatic elements (such as the idea of inexorable Destiny)—this sense, gleaming at intervals from out the darkness of the ancient stage, serves, in the imperfection of its development, to show not the dramatic ability, but the dramatic *in*ability of the ancients." Similarly, in reviewing a volume of old English poetry Poe gave high admiration to Marvell alone, finding in Wotton's famous lines beginning "You meaner beauties of the night" "not one of those higher attributes of Poesy which belong to her under all circumstances and throughout all time" and announcing the general proposition that these older poets are overrated.

It is also especially worth remarking that for one who was generally regarded as iconoclastic, Poe's judgment was in its main outlines strikingly in accordance with the general judgment of the Victorian age. Keats, Shelley, and Coleridge he admired, but he thought Tennyson "the noblest poet who ever lived—*not* because the impressions he produces are, at *all* times, the most profound—*not* because the poetical excitement which he introduces is, at *all* times the most intense—but because it *is*, at all times, the most ethereal—in other words the most elevating and the most pure. No poet is so little of the earth, earthy." And though, for reasons which have already been pointed out, he anathematized Carlyle and everything which smacked of transcendentalism, such deviations as he made from the Victorian standard were more likely to be in the direction of the cheaply sentimental than in the direction of the more austere. Because he himself was so little robust in his passions, he thought Burns "a man whose merits at least have been more grossly—more preposterously exaggerated (through a series of purely adventitious circumstances) than those of any man that ever lived upon the earth," while Thomas Hood is on the contrary "one of the noblest" of modern poets and Tom Moore "the most skillful literary artist of his day,—perhaps any day,— a man who stands in the singular and really wonderful predicament of being undervalued on account of the profusion with which he has scattered about him his good things." "The brilliancies on any one page of 'Lalla Rookh' would have sufficed to establish that very reputation which has been in a great measure selfdimmed by the galaxied lustre of the entire book."

Because of his own limitations the whole body of realistic literature was nearly meaningless to Poe, but he was, on the other hand, easily moved to an exaggerated admiration for whatever seemed to him to adumbrate his own particular interest. Thus Dickens is praised for his "ideality" rather than for the qualities generally attributed to him; *Undine* is ranked as one of the supreme achievements of prose fiction; while *Conti the Discarded; with other Tales and Fancies* by a certain Mr. Chorley is declared to bear "no little resemblance to that purest, and most enthralling of fictions 'the Bride of Lammermuir,'" (*sic*) apparently for no other reason than that it contains passages of melodrama in the manner of *The Mysteries of Udolpho*" and other works of that character.

Poe's especial weakness was, however, for a sort of milk-and-water prettiness into which he appears to have read a meaning related to that ethereal beauty which it was his own desire to create. His idealization of women caused him to be particularly lenient in judging them, and he is thus led into the most extravagant praise of Mrs. Hemans, Mrs. Landon, and their like. "Mrs. Nor-

ton is unquestionably—since the death of Mrs. Hemans—
the Queen of English song"; if she had written nothing
before "this volume would have established her claim
to be the first of living poetesses; but who that is familiar
with the world of song can forget the many gems—rich,
and beautiful, and rare—with which she has spangled
beforetimes her starry crown? . . . The random pieces
which she has poured forth so divinely at intervals, and
which hitherto she has made no effort to preserve, have
found their way into the hearts of all who can be touched
by the mournful or the beautiful, until her name is cherished alike in the humble cottage and the princely hall."

As for the American sisters of these ladies, he was
rarely unable to find in their most abysmally sentimental
effusions some "nobility" or especially some "passionate
purity" to praise. Men were to be slaughtered, but in
women praiseworthy intentions were sufficient defense.
Speaking again of Mrs. Norton and Mrs. Hemans he
writes: "Scarcely a page, moreover, occurs in the writings of either which does not bear testimony to woman's
sufferings and worth. Yes! while it is the fashion to
sneer at the purity of woman's heart, and while a pack
of literary debauchees are libelling our mothers and our
sisters unopposed, from the ranks of that insulted sex
have risen up defenders of its innocence, to shame the
heartless slanderers to silence. Hear in what eloquent
numbers Mrs. Norton vindicates her sex. . . . God bless
her who has written this. The wretches who would rob
the sex of their purity of heart and their uncomplain-
ing endurance of suffering, deserve to die, uncheered by
woman's nurture, unwept by woman's tenderness. Such

beings are not men: they are *aliquid monstri,* monsters in part."

From the example given it is evident that Poe, although he made various penetrating judgments like that embodied in the reviews—especially the first—of Hawthorne, did not have a taste which could be relied upon and that to-day even more than when he wrote there are many of his pronouncements which must seem highly capricious. Moreover, it must be admitted that, in spite of the great stress which he laid upon the necessity for fearless and unprejudiced criticism, he was not himself always above influence. His action in recalling his strictures on Griswold in an effort to patch up their quarrel has already been commented upon, and there are other instances where he changed his opinions in deference to new friendships. To Mrs. Gove Nichols he confessed that need might corrupt him, and according to Mrs. Weiss he said: "You must not judge me by what you find me saying in the magazines. Such expressions of opinion are necessarily modified by a thousand circumstances—the wishes of editors, personal friendships, etc." Yet in spite of all these defects there were reasons why his book-reviewing was of considerable importance.

In the first place he was, especially at the beginning of his career, free from any entangling literary alliances. With the exception of J. P. Kennedy, who had aided him, Poe had no literary friends and hence little reason to do otherwise than speak his mind. He was moreover a Southerner working upon a Southern paper and naturally more inclined than a New Englander would be to rebuke the provinciality of American literature, because to do so cost him no pains to any local pride. If, as has been previously suggested, a natural though not wholly conscious envy inclined him to severity, he was permitted upon most occasions to exercise it and the influence of that severity was generally salutary. Reading him to-day we often feel, as we are bound to feel in reading the reviews of any person of the past who dealt much with the ephemeral literature of his time, that he is more often too lenient than too exigent, since most works lose excellence when seen in the perspective of time; but it was not so that he appeared to his contemporaries. Lowell called him "at once the most discriminating, philosophical, and fearless critic upon imaginative works . . . in America," but he added that Poe "sometimes seems to mistake his phial of prussic acid for his inkstand." In saying that Lowell seems to have expressed a pretty general opinion.

In the second place Poe had an ideal of criticism which he was able to describe even if he could not wholly live up to it, and it is probable that this ideal was not without considerable influence in raising the standard of American periodical criticism. Few if any writers of his time realized as keenly as he did the two opposite but equally malign tendencies of American literary provinciality, and he was perpetually setting himself against both. Sometimes he was scornfully denouncing those who assumed as a matter of course that any European work was better than any native one, but almost as often he was ridiculing the misplaced patriotism which felt it necessary to praise home products merely because they happen to be our own. Just as he endeavored to make

his criticism almost purely aesthetic and, by declaring
moral influence no necessary part of the function of a
work of art, to remove one of the extraneous elements
which affect literary judgment, so too he tried to remove
another such extraneous element by asking that literature be judged wholly on its own merits, without reference to either the servility of the self-conscious provincial
or the obstreperous complacency of the too ardent pa-
triot.

Influence such as that which Poe may have been supposed to have upon American criticism is extremely
difficult to measure. It is certainly very easy to over-
estimate the importance of such elaborate and ostenta-
tious executions as those which he performed upon
literary nonentities who would have died very soon of
their own weakness, and the not infrequent outbursts
of personal animosity which he permitted himself doubtless told against him. To his contemporaries, however,
he seemed both original and highly important and the
service which he performed may be assumed to have been
considerable. Only certain defects prevented it from
being much greater. Partly because of his temperamental predisposition to admire chiefly works of a very
special sort and partly because of his lack of any real
education, he was never able himself to do what he urged
upon American criticism. He could not confront contemporary works with the masterpieces of the past and
dispassionately judge them by the standard of world literature. He was, perhaps, potentially a citizen of the
literary world, an inheritor of the entire culture of the
past; at least he implied that the critic of literature
should be such a one; but because his was, after all, a

mind warped by disease and imperfectly cultivated by education, he was never able to claim that citizenship or to come into that inheritance.

So much, then, may be said of the historical importance of Poe's criticism, but its importance in literature as distinguished from history depends less upon the excellence or the defects of his reviewing than upon the set of principles which he developed to parallel his imaginative writing. This body of doctrine, a moderate aestheticism, has an historical importance of its own, since it set itself squarely against the then prevalent American assumption that literature and piety are twin sisters, and it doubtless played a considerable part in breaking the tyranny of didacticism in American letters. But for the purposes of the present study it must be regarded less in its relation to literary development than in relation to the mind which conceived it.

Before the first of his critiques appeared in the *Messenger* Poe had already begun to produce a new kind of literature, and this fact made it inevitable that, granted the gift of exposition which was his to so striking a degree, he should become a remarkable example of that sort of critic whose function is not primarily judicial. Neither intellectual detachment nor catholicity of taste could be expected of him, but because he had, even when he was least conscious of the fact, his own practice to defend, he was bound to write with passion; and because of his powers of rationalization he could not but formulate with remarkable clarity the principles which he drew from a consideration of his own works. The creations of his imagination satisfy perfectly his critical theories because the theories were made to fit the works; but there are many

EDGAR ALLAN POE

*From a daguerreotype taken by Pratt during Poe's
visit to Richmond*

worse ways than this inductive one for arriving at gener-
alizations which are at least illuminating.

This body of doctrine, first suggested in a preface to
the 1831 volume of poems, developed piecemeal in various
critiques, and finally rather completely summarized in
The Philosophy of Composition and *The Poetic Principle*,
may be briefly stated as follows:[1]

The world of literature is essentially a hierarchy. At
the bottom are the realistic works based upon "that evil
genius of mere matter of fact" against whose "grovelling
and degrading assumptions" it is the duty of the critic to
fight with every weapon in his power (X:30). The
middle ground is occupied by that species of prose tale in
which the artist, "having conceived, with deliberate care,
a certain unique or single *effect* to be wrought out—com-
bines such events as may best aid him in establishing this
preconceived effect" (XI:108), while at the top stands
the true poem.

The tale has a point of superiority even over the poem.
"In fact, while *rhythm* of the latter is an essential aid
in the development of the poet's highest idea—the idea of
the Beautiful—the artificialities of this rhythm are an
inseparable bar to the development of all points of
thought or expression which have their basis in *Truth*.
But Truth is often, and in a very great degree, the aim
of the tale. Some of the finest tales are tales of ratiocination. Thus the field of this species of composition, if
not in so elevated a region on the mountain of mind, is a
tableland of far vaster extent than the domain of the mere

---

[1] The references in parentheses are to volume and page of "The
Complete Works of Edgar Allan Poe: Edited by James A. Harrison."
Though out of print it is the most satisfactory edition.

poem. Its products are never so rich, but infinitely more numerous, and more appreciable by the mass of mankind. . . . The author who aims at the purely beautiful in a prose tale is laboring at a great disadvantage. For Beauty can be better treated in the poem. Not so with terror, or passion, or horror, or a multitude of such other points" (XI: 108–109).

The most exalted species of composition is, however, indisputably that true poetry which may be defined as "The Rhythmical Creation of Beauty" (XIV: 275). From romance it is set off both by the element of rhythm and by the relative vagueness of the incidents with which the emotion is associated, and from a work of science it differs in that it has "for its *immediate* object, pleasure, not truth" (XVI: xliii). The most dangerous of the heresies regarding it is "The Heresy of the Didactic" since poetry has nothing to do with either morality or truth, not because these are unimportant but because it is not in the poem that they are best treated. "The world of the mind" is divided into three departments, that of "Pure Intellect," that of "Taste" and that which is occupied by the "Moral Sense." "Just as the Intellect concerns itself with Truth, so Taste informs us of the Beautiful while the Moral Sense is regardful of Duty. Of this latter, while Conscience teaches the obligation, and Reason the expediency, Taste contents herself with displaying the charms—waging war upon Vice solely on the ground of her deformity—her disproportion—her animosity to the fitting, to the appropriate, to the harmonious—in a word, to Beauty" (XIV: 273).

Man is born with an instinct for this thing called beauty and in the world of nature he finds much to satisfy it. "And just as the lily is repeated in the lake, or the eyes of Amaryllis in the mirror, so is the mere oral or written repetition of these forms, and sounds, and colors, and odors, and sentiments, a duplicate source of delight." Such description is not, however, real poetry because it concerns itself only with the actual and attainable. "He who shall simply sing, with however glowing enthusiasm, or with however vivid a truth of description, of the sights, and sounds and odors and colors, and sentiments, which greet *him* in common with all mankind—he, I say, has yet failed to prove his divine title. There is still a something in the distance which he has been unable to attain. We have still a thirst unquenchable, to allay which he has not shown us the crystal springs. This thirst belongs to the immortality of Man. It is the desire of the moth for the star. It is no mere appreciation of the Beauty before us —but a wild effort to reach the Beauty above. Inspired by an ecstatic prescience of the glories beyond the grave, we struggle, by multiform combinations among the things and thoughts of Time, to attain a portion of that Loveliness whose very elements, perhaps, appertain to eternity alone" (XIV: 273–274).

Because this Beauty is by definition unrealizable, a certain indefiniteness is one of its attributes and thus "Music is the perfection of the soul, or idea, of poetry. The *vagueness* of exaltation aroused by a sweet air (which should be strictly indefinite and never too strongly suggestive) is precisely what we should aim at in poetry" (II: 200). "Affectation, within bounds, is . . . no blemish," but since "ideality" is the supreme attribute of poetry it must never even when dealing with its chief subject, love, be concerned to any great extent with passion.

"It is precisely this 'unpassionate emotion' which is the limit of the true poetical art. Passion proper and poetry are discordant. Poetry, in elevating, tranquilizes the *soul*. With *the heart* it has nothing to do" (XIII: 131). "This [Poetic] Principle itself is, strictly and simply, the Human Aspiration for Supernal Beauty, the manifestation of the Principle is always found in *an elevating excitement of the soul*—quite independent of that passion which is the intoxication of the Heart—or of that Truth which is the satisfaction of the Reason. For, in regard to Passion, alas! its tendency is to degrade, rather than to elevate the Soul. Love, on the contrary—Love—the true, the divine Eros—the Uranian, as distinguished from the Dionæan Venus—is unquestionably the purest and truest of all poetic themes" (XIV: 290). A poem by Mrs. Amelia Welby which deals with regret over a lost lover is good because "her tone is properly subdued, and is not so much a tone of passion as of a gentle and melancholy regret, interwoven with a pleasant sense of the natural loveliness surrounding the lost in the tomb, and a memory of her human beauty while alive. . . . Elegiac poems should either assume this character, or dwell purely on the beauty (moral or physical) of the departed—or, better still, utter the notes of Triumph. I have endeavored to carry out his latter idea in some verses which I have called 'Lenore' . . . A passionate poem is a contradiction in terms" (XVI: 56).

It is impossible that the soul should remain in this state of elevation for more than a short time. "All high excitements are necessarily transient. Thus a long poem is a paradox. And, without unity of impression, the deepest effects cannot be brought about. Epics were the offspring of an imperfect sense of art" (XI: 107). *Paradise Lost* "is to be regarded as poetical, only when, losing sight of that vital requisite in all works of Art, Unity, we view it merely as a series of minor poems. If, to preserve its Unity—its totality of effect or impression—we read it (as would be necessary) at a single sitting, the result is but a constant alternation of excitement and depression. After a passage of what we feel to be true poetry, there follows, inevitably, a passage of platitude which no critical pre-judgment can force us to admire; but if, upon completing the work, we read it again; omitting the first book—that is to say, commencing with the second—we shall be surprised at now finding that admirable which we before condemned—that damnable which we had previously so much admired. . . . But the day of these artistic anomalies is over. If, at any time, any very long poem *were* popular in reality, which I doubt, it is at least clear that no very long poem will ever be popular again." To praise a poet for "sustained effort" is to be guilty of a vulgar error comparable to that of attempting to estimate "Lamartine by the cubic foot, or Pollok by the pound" (XIV: 267–268). Finally, "all experience has shown" that in the highest manifestations of Beauty the "tone is one of *sadness*. Beauty of whatever kind, in its supreme development, invariably excites the sensitive soul to tears. Melancholy is thus the most legitimate of all the poetic tones" (XIV: 198). "This certain taint of sadness is inseparably connected with all the higher manifestations of true Beauty" (XIV: 279), and "When music affects us to tears, seemingly causeless, we weep *not* as Gravina supposes, from 'excess of pleasure'; but through excess of an impatient, petulant sorrow that, as mere mortals, we are as yet in no condition to banquet upon those supernal ecstasies of which the music affords us merely a suggestive and indefinite glimpse" (XVI: 6).

As a result of this analysis of the attributes of supreme beauty it should be possible to discover one subject which satisfies more completely than any other all the requirements, and such is indeed the case. "Now, never losing sight of the object *supremeness,* or perfection, at all points, I asked myself—'Of all melancholy topics, what, according to the *universal* understanding of mankind, is the *most* melancholy?' Death—was the obvious reply. 'And when,' I said, 'is this most melancholy of topics most poetical?' From what I have already explained at some length, the answer, here also is obvious—'When it most closely allies itself to *Beauty*': the death, then, of a beautiful woman, is, unquestionably, the most poetical topic in the world.'"

In considering this body of doctrine, one cannot but be struck, first of all, by the remarkable appearance of logical completeness which it presents, for once its premises are granted the conclusions are drawn with the same elaborate clarity which is characteristic of Poe's ratiocinative tales. In the second place, it is evident that they do contain certain elements of truth. The definition of Beauty does at least describe very clearly a kind of beauty, and thus though the doctrines may not have the universality claimed for them, they do succeed in doing in their own way all that the best set of critical principles has ever done, which is, not to lay down the laws which govern all art, but to define, as accurately as is possible, a style. Yet it is certainly a work of supererogation to point out that this definition is merely a description of the effect which Poe himself was endeavoring to produce, and since his art was the result of an unrecognized and uncontrollable need, it must follow that the criticism is, like the thing criticised, the product not of the abstract reason of which Poe was so proud but of the forces which led him into a system of rationalization which became ever more complex.

The sources of his criticism have been frequently discussed. It has often been stated that his master was Coleridge and the statement is true—in so far as he had any master except himself. Thus in the preface to the 1831 volume the central doctrine was expressed as follows: "A poem, in my opinion, is opposed to a work of science by having, for its *immediate* object, pleasure, not truth." If we compare this with the statement of Coleridge that "A poem is that species of composition which is opposed to works of science, by proposing for its immediate object not truth," it will appear that Poe's only contribution is to be found in the phrase "in my opinion." Yet it is not to be supposed that the youthful poet, after a thorough course of study in aesthetics, had decided to make his works conform to the theories of Coleridge. Nothing is more characteristic of his mind than the pertinacity with which he held to a useful phrase or a fact upon which he had chanced to fall, and he needed no more than a hint such as he got in this sentence from Coleridge or in Bacon's dictum concerning beauty and strangeness to set him off upon a line of thought which led him through numerous by-paths until it seemed to cover the universe. Coleridge's remark was true because there was need to defend his non-moral art in a country where literature was generally considered the handmaiden of utilitarian ethics, just as Bacon's was true because the beauty which Poe himself created had always that element of strangeness. Taking the two together he could prove that his own work was pure and perfect, and the hidden spring of energy behind his critical writing was the desire to do just that.

What had been said of the central principle of his aesthetic may be said with equal truth of all its details. It may be, as has been suggested, that his idea of brevity as essential to a true poem was taken from Schlegel, but the fact, vouched for by Mrs. Weiss, that he was himself incapable of sustained effort is surely of more significance in accounting for the existence of the idea than any German source whatsoever. So too his assertion that the highest beauty is always passionless and always melancholy is less the result of a logical deduction than of the fact that to him passion was always repellent and the highest pleasure shadowed by sadness. Because he did not himself realize what it was that he sought, a vagueness like music is inseparable from the highest poetry, and, finally and most specifically, because only unattainable women could move without maddening him, "The most poetic of all ideas is the death of a beautiful woman."

Poe's criticism is, then, as intensely personal as his poetry or his fiction. Beauty as he defines it includes nothing except beauty of the sort which he himself produced. And the primary value of the criticism is as an interpretation, not of literature in general, but of his own works.

It must be remembered, moreover, that however true this interpretation may be upon the level of art it is upon the level of psychology either false or at least misleading. The logic with which he supports his principles is not the product of a free mind but an elaborate rationalization whose real function is to support a predetermined taste; the character of the satisfaction which his contemplation of "the beautiful" produces is not such as he sees it and describes it—a sort of intimation of that beauty which lies beyond human apprehension—but instead a balm to wounded nerves; and while he is related to those French decadents who acknowledge to a greater extent than he does the psychological meaning of their temperaments, he creates for his works a different significance by inventing an aesthetic which assigns to them new values. Thus his criticism is not only an analysis of his own work but an analysis made by one who did not fully understand the genesis of the thing analyzed and was unconsciously eager to disguise its origin from himself as well as from others.

The test of practice proves, what the circumstances of its origin would lead one to expect, that Poe's doctrine can have no standing as a comprehensive theory of aesthetic. It would exclude too much from the body of world literature and it would discount too much of major importance, while it exalts minor works to a preëminence which they could have only for those whose temperament was somehow abnormal like his. Judged by his principles the *Odyssey* would be, as Andrew Lang points out, inferior to *Ulalume*, and *Le Festin de Pierre* to *Undine*. Moreover, since Poe's banishment of morality from art is not merely a protest against didacticism but implies also that even as *themes*, moral ideas must be excluded, it follows that all works of the highest art must be, like his own, very remote from human life. As Lang said in another essay: "To any one who believes that the best, the immortal poetry, is nobly busied with great actions and great passion, Poe's theory seems fatally narrow. Without the conceptions of duty and truth we can have no *Antigone* and no *Prometheus*. The great and paramount ideas have always been the inspirers of honorable actions, and by following them men and women are led into the dramatic situations which are the materials of Shakespeare, Aeschylus, and Homer. There is an immortal strength in the stories of great actions, but Poe in theory and practice disdains all action and rejects this root of immortality. He deliberately chooses fantasy for his portion. Now, while it is not the business of poetry to go about distributing tracts, she can never neglect actions and situations which under her spell become unconscious lessons of morality." And this is essentially true, even though one does not demand that poetry should inculcate even "unconscious lessons of morality," since moral ideas, true or false, are the source of many of the most exalted passions which poetry can utilize.

. . . .

We have, then, traced Poe's art to an abnormal condition of the nerves and his critical ideas to a rationalized defense of the limitations of his own taste. We have also indicated that even as an interpretation of his own works his criticism falls short of psychological truth and it might seem that we had thus undertaken to destroy the value of his work. Such is far, however, from being the intention. The question whether or not the case of Poe represents an exaggerated example of the process by which all creation is performed is at least an open question. The extent to which all imaginative works are the result of the unfulfilled desires which spring from either idiosyncratic or universally human mal-adjustments to life is only beginning to be investigated, and with it is linked the related question of the extent to which all critical principles are at bottom the systematized and rationalized expression of instinctive tastes which are conditioned by causes often unknown to those whom they affect. The problem of finding an answer to these questions and of determining what effect, if any, the findings in any particular case should have upon the evaluation of the works of imagination or interpretation so produced, is the one distinctly new problem which the critic of to-day is called upon to consider. He must, in a word, endeavor to find the relationship which exists between psychology and aesthetics, but since the present state of knowledge is not such as to enable anyone satisfactorily to determine that relationship, we must proceed only with the greatest caution and content ourselves with saying that the fallacy of origins, that species of false logic by which a thing is identified with its ultimate source, is nowhere more dangerous than in the realm of art, and criticism is, at times at least, much more of an art than a science.

Whatever a critic can convincingly read into a work may be said to be actually there, even though it be thought of as the creation of the critic rather than of the author criticised. And the works of Poe have his own interpretations of them as one of the various modes in which they exist. They have been read in the light of his intention and the effect which they have produced has been at least so modified by that intention as to be different from the effect which they would have produced had he and his readers been aware of the psychological processes behind them. That legend of himself which he fashioned in a manner so marvelously inclusive that it employs as material everything from the events of his daily life to the products of his imagination is finally completed by his interpretation. His criticism inscribes a curve within which everything else is included; it unifies all the various aspects of his life and work; and thus it makes his legend as a whole, rather than any of the individual stories or poems which are but a part of it, his supreme artistic creation.

INDEX

INDEX

INDEX

240

INDEX

Irving, 152, 155
Israfel, 67, 96

James, 195
Jefferson, 27

Keats, 65, 206, 218
Kennedy, 41, 44, 45, 46, 63, 64, 221.
Kent, 18
Kepler, 185
King Pest, 82
Koran, The, 96

Lalla Rookh, 96, 219
Lamartine, 229
Landon, 66, 143, 219
Landor, 165
Lang, 95, 233, 234.
Laplace, 93
Latrobe, 41
Lemaître, 209
"Lenore," 61, 67, 120, 228.
Letters on Natural Magic, 102
Lewis, 188
Ligeia, 24, 75, 76, 77, 117, 125
Literary Character, 96
Literary Gazette, 155, 158
Littérature de tout á l'heure, 96
Literati, The, 146, 159
Living Age, The, 155, 158
Longfellow, 89, 132, 133, 135, 138,
    140, 143, 144, 148, 155, 161, 192,
    194, 197
Longstreet, 216
Lowell, 89, 130, 138, 145, 152, 155,
    161, 192, 194, 197, 212, 222
Lynch, Charlotte, 164

McMurtrie, 141
Madeline, 24, 125
Maelzel's Chess-Player, 99, 107
Mallarmé, 200, 207, 209
Man of the Crowd, The, 126
Ms. Found in a Bottle, 42, 68
Marginalia, 96, 159
Markham, 17
Marvell, 218
Mary, 40, 52
Masque of the Red Death, The, 77

Mattson, 89
Mesmeric Revelation, 158
Messenger Star, The, 134
Midnight Mass for the Dying
    Year, 144
Miller, 41
Modern Language Notes, 214
Moore, 96, 143, 219
Moran, 3, 4
More, 193, 195
Morella, 24, 75, 76, 77, 125
Morice, 208
Morris, 164
Motherwell, 145
Motley, 155
Murders in the Rue Morgue, The,
    102, 103, 108, 152, 200
Mysteries of Udolpho, The, 219

Narrative of Arthur Gordon Pym,
    The, 69, 201
National Magazine, 158
Neal, 165
Newton, 183
New York Review, 95
Noah, 131, 133
Norman Leslie, 214
Norton, 143, 219, 220

O'Brien, 204
Ode on a Grecian Flute, 160
Odyssey, 233
Oedipus at Colonos, 93
Osgood, 57, 131, 164, 167, 168, 170,
    171, 173, 180
"Outis," 145

Paracelsus, 154
Paradise Lost, 135, 229
Passaic, 164
Paul Ulric, 89
Péladan.
Philadelphia Saturday Museum,
    148
Philosophy of Composition, The,
    98, 113, 115, 118, 225
Pinikidia, 96
Pit and the Pendulum, The, 78
Plato, 209

241

INDEX

INDEX